The Oath and Perjury in Ancient Greece

The Oath and Perjury in Ancient Greece

Joseph Plescia

Florida State University Press
Tallahassee / 1970

A Florida State University Press Book

LIBRARY OF CONGRESS CATALOG CARD NO. 79-94804

PRINTED BY THE E. O. PAINTER PRINTING COMPANY
DE LAND, FLORIDA

Preface

THE OATH," says Lycurgus, the great Athenian orator of the fourth century B.C., "is the power that holds democracy together; the state is constituted of three parts, the archon, the judge, and the private citizen; each of these takes the oath as a pledge and rightly so." There is hardly a speech by the Athenian orators wherein the oath is not mentioned for one reason or another, and there is no doubt that it played an important role in the law and life of the Greeks.

The purpose of the following study is to trace the historical development of the oath in ancient Greece and to discuss the nature of the various oaths as used primarily by the Athenians. However, its emphasis lies on the legal rather than the religious aspect of the oath. Specifically, the work aims to offer a comprehensive view of the oath with a historical analysis in order to present it in its proper perspective.

Since the span of the Greek history, ranging from the advent of the Achaeans to the encroachment of the Romans, is so vast, the scope of this work is limited to the period from Homer to Aristotle, though references will be made to later ages of Greek history whenever the nature of the events and documents bears upon the arguments under discussion.

In regard to the translations I used the following procedure. For long passages I availed myself, in most cases, of established translations, such as B. Jowett's *The Dialogues of Plato,* E. Barker's *The Politics of Aristotle,* G. W. Botsford's and E. G. Sihler's *Hellenic Civilization,* K. J. Maidment's *Adocides' On the Mysteries,* J. Frazer's *Pausanias' Description of Greece,* R. J. Bonner's and G. Smith's *The oath of the Hieromnemoi,* and others. For short passages I endeavoured to provide my own translations, always, however, consulting other versions, such as C. R. Kennedy's *The Orations of Demosthenes,* and especially the Loeb Classical Library on account of its accessibility and comprehensiveness. I would like to take this opportunity to acknowledge my debt to all these sources and to the various publishers who kindly granted permission for passages to be quoted.

I am indebted to many of my colleagues for criticism and advice, but I must acknowledge specifically Professor James Preu, Director of the Florida State University Press, and his staff for their invaluable editorial help. I am also grateful to Professors Leon Golden and Vincent Thursby for their encouragement in the early stages of the manuscript and to the reader for his excellent suggestions. Naturally errors of fact and judgment that may remain in the monograph are my own responsibility.

Tallahassee, 1969. JOSEPH PLESCIA

Table of Contents

ONE

The Oath-Formula

EVERY SOCIETY DEVELOPS MEANS by which it tries to maintain itself. In its early stages, when concepts of social ethics and legal norms were still primitive because social conscience, from which those principles were derived, was still in its infancy, the forces that bound people together were essentially coercive. It was power that people most feared and to such a degree that they eventually developed a complex of religious rites and ceremonies. So, early organized societies were basically religious; the divine power was felt to be immediate, ever present and ever active, and the oath was one of the socio-religious acts which to a great extent governed the interrelationships of men at this level of development. An analysis of the concept of the oath-formula, therefore, will be necessary before the discussion explores its development and uses in the various stages and aspects of life in ancient Greek society.

The Greek word most frequently translated into English as "oath" is *horkos*. *Horkos* and its synonym *herkos* mean, etymologically,[1] "fence," "enclosure," "that which confines or constrains."

1. E. Boisacq, "Horkos," *Dictionnaire Étymologique de la Langue Grecque*, 4th ed. (Heidelberg, 1950).

And since the oath was an aspect of social justice, *horkion* (that which is sworn) was equivalent to *dikaion* (that which is right).[2] *Horkos* is also a cognate of *exorkismos* (exorcism), which puts evil things and persons "outside the fence" and, therefore, outside the protection of the gods. J. L. Myres,[3] furthermore, relates the concept of *horkos* to the Roman *obligatio* and *religio*: "The Roman *obligatio*," he says, "is a 'tethering' of a man so that he cannot stray and run risks; a reinforcement of that internal restraint on conduct for which the Roman word is *religio*."

The following are some of the most common Greek expressions which indicated the taking of the oath: (a) *omnymi* (to confirm by oath) and its compounds, e.g., *pro-omnymi* (to swear first), *antomnymi* (to counter-swear), *diomnymi* (to swear solemnly), etc.; (b) *horkoō* or *horkizō* (to bind by oath); (c) the compounds *euorkeō* (to take a true oath), *epiorkeō* (to foreswear oneself); (d) the phrases *pistin didonai, lambanein, poieisthai* (to tender, to accept, and to exchange oaths respectively) ; note here that *pistis* (faith) is a synonym of *horkos*; (e) *spondas* or *horkia temnein* (to cut the victims); obviously, the implication in this last case is that the oaths were sealed by sacrifices and libations.

In its religious meaning, the oath was an invocation to a deity as a witness to the truth of a statement made by the oath-taker and a surety or avenger of a promise broken. Therefore, it was believed that a man spoke by the authority of the gods invoked in the oath and that the gods guaranteed the words of such a man. In fact, in the *Iliad* (3, 278 and 7, 76 respectively), the gods in whose names the oaths were sworn are called *martyroi* (witnesses) and *epi martyroi* (sureties):

οἳ ὑπένερθε καμόντας
ἀνθρώπους τίνυσθον, ὅτις κ' ἐπίορκον ὀμόσσηι,
ὑμεῖς μάρτυροι ἔστε, φυλάσσετε δ' ὅρκια πιστά.

(You who under the earth take vengeance on dead men, whoever among them has sworn falsely, you shall be *witnesses*, and shall guard the binding oaths.)

ὧδε δὲ μυθέομαι, Ζεὺς δ'ἄμμ' ἐπὶ μάρτυρος ἔστω.

(I make the following terms, and let Zeus be a *surety*.)

2. Diogenes Laertius, 8, 33.
3. J. L. Myres, *The Political Ideas of the Greeks* (New York, 1927), p. 209.

In *Oedipus the King* (646-7 and 652), Sophocles adds that the gods invoked in the oath are offended not only when one gives a false oath, but also when one simply refuses to believe another's oath:

> ὦ πρὸς θεῶν πίστευσον, Οἰδίπους, τάδε,
> μάλιστα μὲν τόνδ' ὅρκον αἰδεσθεὶς θεῶν.
>
> (For the sake of the gods, Oedipus, believe these things, and especially the oath, for fear of the gods.)
>
> τὸν οὔτε πρὶν νήπιον νῦν τ'ἐν ὅρκωι μέγαν καταίδεσαι.
>
> (Respect him who has never been foolish in the past and who now is strong in his oath.)

In ancient Greek society, the oath generally included the following three elements: (1) a solemn declaration of truth or of promise, (2) an invocation of god or gods to guarantee such a declaration, and (3) a religious sanction (independent of human justice) in the form of a curse, in case the person taking the oath perjures himself. Accordingly, the Greek oath may properly be defined as follows: *an outward pledge by the oath-taker that his attestation or promise is made under an immediate sense of responsibility to a god or gods.*[4] Sometimes, however, the religious oath referred only to the curse on oneself, on one's relatives or property, which automatically struck the oath-taker in case of perjury, that is, by the magical power of the words.

In its general meaning, the oath was merely a solemn affirmation or promise, which bound one's own conscience before the civil authority, other people, or even before oneself. Such an oath, in which the invocation of the divinity and the curse were no longer essential, was made either on one's honor or life. In this monograph, however, we are concerned only with the Greek oath as defined above, that is, in its religious sense.

According to the Greeks, then, the obligation to keep the oath was felt to be absolute, that is, to be fulfilled at all cost. According to Hesiod (*Theogony* 793-803), even a god who had perjured himself could not escape the curse of the oath; it was believed that he would fall into a deep sleep and be deprived of his divinity for a

4. H. C. Black, "Oath," *Law Dictionary*, 4th ed. (St. Paul, Minn., 1951). Also, R. Hirzel, *Der Eid* (Leipzig, 1902), pp. 1-7 and 11 f.

number of years. "There is," says Empedocles (frag. B115),[5] "an oracle of Necessity, an ancient decree of the gods, eternal, sealed fast with mighty oaths: when someone sinfully stains his own limbs with bloodshed and swears a false oath, the divine spirits, who live a long life, force him to wander for thrice ten thousand seasons far from the company of the blessed ones, being born, throughout the period, into all kinds of mortal shapes, changing from one hard way of life to another."

It is not surprising, moreover, that the Greek mind, so prone to transform forces and ideas into anthropomorphic myths, that is, with its mythopoetic bent, introduced under the name *Horkos* a special daimonic being. In fact, this was a god of the underworld, whose function was to receive the perjurer into the infernal regions of Hades and punish him. In the *Works and Days* (803f) Hesiod not only makes *Horkos* the son of *Eris* (Strife), evidently because oaths often came up in disputes, but also associates *Horkos* with the Erinyes, the goddesses of revenge, whose duty was precisely to punish the one on whom the revenge of *Horkos* had fallen, namely, the perjurer.

There is, however, some dispute about the god or gods to be properly invoked in the oath. For migratory peoples, just as their dwelling places were undetermined and of little importance, so, too, their gods were vague, simply *dynameis* (powers), and of little importance. Thus, for the invading Achaeans and Dorians the gods were universal—the ever present *Zeus* (Sky), *Ge* (Earth), and all-seeing *Helios* (Sun). Accordingly, the formula of the oath for them was also universal and simple: *Ne Dia* or *Ma Dia* (Yes, by God, or No, by God);[6] and the god so conceived was called rather as a witness than an avenger of perjury. It was up to the wronged man to avenge himself.

When eventually the tribes settled down, portions of land (*temene*) were dedicated to the gods, who, thus, settled down also. Soon these tribes became independent political units and the gods became the local lords, around whom the community rallied: *cuius regio, eius religio* (wherever his region, there his cult). Then, the formula of the oath also became local, particular: *Ne ton Dia tou-*

5. G. S. Kirk and J. E. Raven, *The Presocratic Philosophers* (Cambridge, Eng., 1960), pp. 351-52.

6. E. Ziebarth, *De Jurejurando in Jure Graeco Quaestiones* (Göttingen, 1892). Also, G. Glotz, "Jusjurandum," *Darem.-Saglio.*

toni or *Ma ton Dia toutoni* (Yes, by the God of this place or No, by the God of this place),[7] that is, god plus epithet. Thus, the gods so invoked in the oath-formula were connected with a specific place or local object, such as a stone, tree, altar, or temple.

From the period of the codification of the laws, with its principal concern to determine more clearly the rules of procedure, two types of oath-formula began to develop in Greece: the private and the official.

Apparently, there were no legal restrictions to determine the formula of the private oath. As a general rule, however, the number and the names of the gods varied according to the circumstances of place, time, age, and sex of the oath-taker; each group, each guild, each social class had its own *theoi horkioi* (oath-gods), and there was a certain relationship between the gods invoked and the group; that is, people swore by those gods who had jurisdiction over their professions or over their lives. Thus, the custom grew that courtesans swore by Aphrodite, soldiers swore by Ares, and physicians by Apollo the Healer; in short, the members of various professional associations swore by their protecting gods or hero-gods, to whom they had sworn allegiance, and who, thus, constituted the cohesive force among the members. Similarly, just as the slaves swore by their human-masters, so the freemen swore by their god-masters.

If, in private life, the oath-gods were not to be taken at random, but were to be determined by custom, this was even more the case in public life. The gods had to be local (*enchorioi*) and officially recognized (*nomimoi*), i.e., enjoying the public worship. So, each independent community determined its own local and legal formula (*enchorios kai nomimos horkos*), its own oath-gods (*theoi horkioi*) by whom the citizens had to swear. According to Thucydides (2, 71, 4), for example, when at the beginning of the Peloponnesian War the Spartans marched against Plataea, the Plataeans reminded them of the oath by their national gods, taken by Pausanias and the allies soon after the Persian War, to guarantee the independence of Plataea in the future. Said the Plataeans: "Appealing to the oath-gods, in whose names we then swore, *both the gods of your ancestors and the gods of our own country*, we tell you not to harm the land of Plataea, nor to break the oaths, but to allow us to live independently, as Pausanias justly decided."

7. E. Ziebarth, "Eid," *RE*. Also, G. Glotz, "Jusjurandum," *Darem.-Saglio*.

In another passage, apparently quoting the original document of the alliance-treaty between Athens and Argos, Thucydides (5, 47, 8) again emphasized the fact that the parties swore by their national oath-gods: "Each party shall swear by the oath which is most binding in his own country over full-grown sacrificial victims."

The number of gods invoked by name in the official oath varied; the number three seems to have been most commonly used until the end of the fourth century B.C. The Athenians,[8] for instance, generally swore by the triad Zeus-Apollo-Demeter; the Phocians[9] swore by the triad Apollo-Leto-Artemis; but the Olympians[10] swore by one god—Zeus Olympios; and the Ozolian Locrians[11] made a place for themselves with their oath by five gods (the *Pentorkia*), whose names are not known to us with certainty.

In treaties between equal sovereign states, the parties jealously swore their own local and legal oath in accordance with the customs of the fatherland.[12] However, Athens, when she turned her first league (founded in 477 B.C.) into an empire, began to impose her oath-gods (*theoi horkioi*) or legal oath (*nomimos horkos*) on her subject allies. This obtrusion might be explained as an attempt to enforce religious allegiance, and thereby give religious sanction to her hegemony.[13]

Occasionally, the parties put their oath-gods together into one single formula: "The idea," says E. Ziebarth,[14] "was now obvious, like the states themselves the gods also were brought closer to one another in a treaty, wherein a new common formula, which both parties swore, was established from the two local legal oaths." This custom became common from the second half of the fourth century B.C. By this time, also, the formula began to include all the local gods that could be remembered and to end with the all-inclusive invocation of the rest of the gods and goddesses. The great number of the invoked gods forbids individual mention of them here. A Cretan formula, for instance, invokes as many as seventeen.[15]

During the Hellenistic period, with the establishment of the

8. M. N. Tod, *A Selection of Greek Historical Inscriptions*, 2 vols. (Oxford, 1946-48), nos. 29 and 127.

9. *Syll.*,[3] 145.

10. Pausanias, 5, 24, 9.

11. Tod, 34.

12. Thucydides, 5, 18, 9; 5, 47, 8.

13. For details see Chapter Four.

14. Ziebarth, "Eid," *RE*.

15. *Ibid.*

dynasts, the oath by the new lords (*basilikos horkos*) who replaced, or better identified themselves with the old gods, became common. The Greeks, therefore, were historically prepared, when the Roman Empire appeared, to take oaths by the *Genius* of the Emperor.

In conclusion, as a general rule, no one swore by a deity not having a shrine in the city; the oath-gods had to be local and legally recognized; in treaties between equal sovereign states, each party swore its own local and legal oath according to the ancestral customs.

This local connection of the oath-gods raises two questions. The first is whether these state-gods were considered to be universal or strictly local. Fustel de Coulanges[16] stated without ambiguity that the state-gods were strictly local: "But because two cities happened to give the same name to their god, we are not to conclude that they worshipped the same god. There was an Athene at Athens and there was one at Sparta; but they were two different goddesses . . . because the ancients did not attribute the gift of ubiquity to the gods. The cities of Argos and Samos had each a Here Polias, but it was not the same goddess, for she was represented in the two cities with two different attributes."

In this paragraph, Fustel de Coulanges presents two arguments for the localization of the Greek gods. One is based on the principle of ubiquity, that is, the gods were not everywhere at the same time. Therefore, they could not hear and protect everybody at the same time. The other is based on the use of epithets, that is to say, the epithet is not only descriptive, but also distinctive. Therefore, the epithet-name distinguished one god from another, though the first name could have been identical. In conclusion, according to Fustel de Coulanges, the Athene of Athens was an entirely different goddess from the Athene of Sparta, though they might have performed similar functions.

M. P. Nilsson,[17] on the other hand, seems to believe that the Greek gods, who were universal at the beginning, remained so, even though they later assumed different functions and epithets in various states: "The Athene of Athens was the same goddess as the

16. N. D. Fustel de Coulanges, *La Cité Antique,* 22nd ed. (Paris, 1912), p. 175.

17. M. P. Nilsson, *Geschichte der Griechischen Religion*, 2 vols (Munich, 1941-50), vol. 1, p. 678. Also, J. W. Jones, *The Law and Legal Theory of the Greeks* (Oxford, 1956), p. 98.

Athene of Thebes. . . . The Athenian Athene could not go into battle against the Theban Athene."

According to Victor Ehrenberg,[18] there was a leading local god and, around him, a horde of more or less subordinate deities who enjoyed state worship. The leading local god "took the place of the king; he became monarch of a state that had ceased to be monarchical. . . . It was . . . a very general practice to ascribe the permanent leadership of a state to a god as 'leader' (*archegetes*)."

In conclusion, regarding the first question whether the state-gods were local or universal, the evidence and the conflicting theories suggest this evolution: in the nomadic stage, the gods were probably universal, but, as soon as the various tribes settled down, a process of differentiation, due to isolation and inward oriented consolidation, took place. Such a differentiation, naturally, also affected religion, gods, and rites. However, when later the individual communities began to look outward, promoting commerce and colonization, then the poets started a process of syncretizing the different gods, so that in literature we witness certain degrees of identification among the gods, but officially and among the masses the state-gods kept their local individuality, which lasted as long as the city-states kept theirs, for political independence also implied religious autonomy.[19] Furthermore, certain local individualization is inherent in the nature of polytheism.

The second question, raised by the local connection of the gods, concerns the relationship between the community and its guardian god (*polieus*) or goddess (*polias*). For the Greeks the gods who protected the state and were revered as its divine leaders were the representatives of the historical life of the community.[20] They did not conceive the state as a corporation in the modern sense of the word, that is, as a legal person, but as a community whose life depended on its guardian god; thus Athens was, as it were, held in trust by the goddess Athene. Therefore, in ancient Greek communities religion was not only a theological and psychological, but also a juridical conception.[21] This was, of course, theocracy. But we must hasten to note that the Greek theocracy

18. V. Ehrenberg, *The Greek State* (New York, 1960), pp. 16-19.

19. J. W. Jones, *op. cit.*, p. 94.

20. Paul Vinogradoff, *Outline of Historical Jurisprudence*, II (Oxford, 1922), p. 106.

21. Vinogradoff, *op. cit.*, p. 98.

differed from the oriental theocracy in that in the oriental the power of the ruler came directly from the state-gods, whereas in the Greek theocracy the power of the magistrates came from the state-gods through the people; hence, in the latter, sovereignty (*kratos*) really resided in the people and in the state-gods.

The state authority, then, was simply the concrete expression of the will of both the citizen assembly by direct representation and the state-god or gods, whose will, in fact, the citizens sought before all public activities by sacrifices, omens, and oracles. The citizen assembly, as the political ruler, and the god of the state, as the divine king, were brought together in what expressed the will of both, in the law (*nomos*), which really became "*Nomos the King*."[22]

In conclusion, in regard to the second question concerning the relationship between the community and its guardian god or gods, one can say that the oath-gods of the local and legal oath-formula were juridical persons and the lords of the state. In fact, they not only owned, inherited, bought, and sold property, but also, as juridical persons they played the part of the buyer in the sale-contract of the manumission of slaves.[23]

Although the Greeks swore oaths by their local deities, whom they considered as juridical persons, the rites of swearing were fairly uniform among the various city-states and the evolution of the ceremonies followed a similar pattern. Customarily, the official oaths were taken beside a sacred precinct. In the early periods this might have been, for instance, a rock, a tree or a spring.[24] At Athens, even down to the fourth century B.C., the archons took their oath of investiture on the so-called Rock of Oaths. However, when the Greeks turned their cities into groves of beautiful temples, these became the most common places in which they took oaths. Not surprisingly, the temples were often built on ground previously considered sacred.

The oath was taken standing up, with the arms outstretched and touching the sacred object with which the invoked god was connected: "by the god of this place" (*ma ton theon toutoni*).[25]

Generally speaking, there was no important oath without a

22. V. Ehrenberg, *op. cit.*, p. 98.
23. J. W. Jones, *op. cit.*, p. 284.
24. J. G. Frazer, *Pausanias' Description of Greece*, 2nd ed., 6 vols. (London, 1913), vol. 2, p. 364 (bk. 1, 28, 5); vol. 4, p. 253 (bk. 8, 18, 4).
25. Glotz, "Jusjurandum," *Darem.-Saglio.*

sacrifice and a libation. In the early periods, the sacrifice followed the oath and was, as it were, a *mise en scène* of the curse. Later, from about the seventh century B.C., the sacrifice preceded the oath and represented the purification rite before the invocation of the oath god; the oath was taken on the victim, which united the invoked god with the oath-taker by a sacred power, while the burned victim itself became, in a way, the symbol of the curse.[26]

An example of oath-sacrifice is the account of Pausanias (3, 20, 9) concerning the oath of Helen's suitors: "Going on, we came to a place called the Horse's Tomb. For here Tyndareus sacrificed a horse and swore the suitors of Helen, making them stand on the pieces of the horse. The oath was to defend Helen and him who might be chosen to marry her, if ever they should be wronged. Having sworn them, he buried the horse here."[27]

Another instance is the oath ceremony of the Achaean armada before sailing against Troy. The soothsayer Calchas brought a boar into the market place and divided it into two parts. Then each man, with drawn sword in hand, passed between the two pieces of the boar, while the blade of his sword was smeared with its blood. Thus they swore enmity to Priam. According to J. G. Frazer, the explanation of such a ceremony is probably that the parties of the oath were believed to be taken "within the mystical life of the victim."[28]

As an illustration from the classical period of such an oath-sacrifice, Demosthenes (23, 68) reports that in trials before the court of the Areopagus at Athens, the plaintiff had to take an oath, and that he was "not to consider this oath as an ordinary oath, but as one which no man swears for any other occasion, for he stands over the entrails of a boar, a ram and a bull; and these must have been slaughtered by the appointed officials and on certain determined days, so that in respect both of the time and of the officials, all the sacred ceremonies have been satisfied."

Often, certain actions accompanied the sacrifice; for instance, the parties of an alliance grasped hands; Aristotle (*Const. of Athens*, 23, 5) says that Aristides threw bars of iron into the sea

26. J. G. Frazer, *op. cit.*, vol. 3, 367 (bks. 3, 20, 9; 4, 15, 8; 5, 24, 9).

27. Trans. J. G. Frazer, *op. cit.*, vol. 1, p. 167.

28. J. G. Frazer, *op. cit.*, vol. 3, pp. 367-68. For a similar view concerning the magic union of the oath-taker with the victim see M. P. Nilsson, *op. cit.*, vol. 1, pp. 54 and 128-29.

to symbolize that the Delian league was to be perennial:[29] "and [he] administered the oaths to the Ionians so that they should have the same friends and enemies; thereupon they also dropped iron bars into the sea." According to Plutarch (*Dion*, 56, 3), in Syracuse, the person who takes the 'great oath' (*megan horkon*) "enters into the sanctuary of Demeter and Persephone, where, after certain rites have been performed, he puts on the purple vestment of the goddess, takes a burning torch in his hand and recites the oath." This amounted to attaching the oath to a sacrilege, the pardon for which could not be obtained, except by fulfilling the oath at all costs.

Another custom was that of the soldiers before they went into battle: they took the blood of the victim and dipped their hands and swords into it, thereby giving evidence that they were all bound together, each man to each.[30]

Evidently, such ceremonies were also a form of publicity before gods and men. The publicity was necessary for the validity of the actions, because at a time when there were not yet any written records, it provided witnesses for them.

To take an oath, then, was to impose upon oneself a law, the sanction of which was the curse. The oath, said the oracle of Delphi, has a son, nameless and, though without hands and feet, swift to pursue and certain in grip, making an end of a man's house and race;[31] the curse unfailingly reached the perjurer, even in the afterlife.

The sanction, that is, the curse, was in the form of a contract with the invoked god; in it the oath-taker gave as evidence of his *bona fides* pledges which he undoubtedly would forfeit in case of perjury. Its formulae varied according to the type of oath and the class of people. For instance, a soldier would have sworn by, that is, given as pledge, his weapons, a married woman her matrimonial bed, a king his royal scepter, and a father his children, household, or even his own life. Originally, in cases of treason, the man who had perjured himself was considered to have been consecrated to the invoked god so that anyone could have killed him with impunity.

29. Compare Herodotus' reference (1, 165) to the oath of the Phocaeans when they chose to emigrate rather than to submit to the yoke of the Persians: "then they dropped a bar of iron into the sea and swore never to return to Phocaea until it floated up again."

30. J. G. Frazer, *op. cit.*, vol. 3, p. 367.

31. Herodotus, 6, 86.

The degree of solemnity and sacredness of the oath was, therefore, determined by the latitude and gravity of the curse. The most common curse-formulae found in the orators were: (1) to swear on the lives of the children or to place imprecation upon the children;[32] (2) to swear by full-grown victims;[33] (3) to imprecate destruction upon oneself, one's kindred, and one's house.[34] This last formula is generally found in the most grave occasions, such as in capital and heavy fine cases, and it is known as *diomosia*.

The curse, as already indicated, was intimately connected with the sacrifice and libations. According to Pausanias (5, 24, 10), the ancient Greeks believed that it was a divine law that a sacrificial animal, on which an oath had been taken, should not be eaten by man; and in support of this belief Pausanias refers to a passage in the *Iliad* (19, 261ff), where Homer describes how a sacrificed boar, on which Agamemnon swore that he truly had never laid hand on Briseis with the intention of taking her to bed with him, was hurled by the herald into the sea:

> So he spoke, and with pitiless bronze he cut the boar's throat.
> Talthybios swung the body around and cast it into the deep
> Of the grey sea, a food for fish.

Eustathius,[35] commenting on Homer, remarked that the sacrificial victims, upon which the oaths were taken, were by some people buried in the earth, by others cast into the sea, it being wholly forbidden to partake of them. This, perhaps, may be explained by the fact that the victim was believed to have been polluted or "consecrated" by the curse.

The destruction of the victim symbolized the fate of the perjurer. The sacrifice was, in fact, a conditional curse: The oath-taker wished, in the event he did not keep the oath, to be struck like the victim which he had killed. Furthermore, by touching the victim, the oath-taker identified himself with it, and the curse, which was now, in a concrete form, in the victim, would transfer to the oath-taker by this contact if he did not state the truth. The sacrifice, therefore, had a magic character and touching the sacri-

32. Dem. 29, 26, 33, 54; 54, 40. Lysias, 32, 13.
33. Dem. 59, 60.
34. Dem. 23, 67; 54, 40.
35. J. G. Frazer, *op. cit.*, vol. 3, p. 640 (bk. 5, 24, 10).

ficial victim permitted the transfer (in a potential form) of the curse to the oath-taker.[36]

Finally, mention must be made of the fact that, when the oath-taker swore rightly, he claimed a reward for his truthfulness; for the oath, and, for that matter, all relationships with the gods, were in the form of a contract. A very simple and common formula ran as follows: faithful to my oath, may I prosper; perjurer, may misfortune befall me.

The examination of the concept of the oath per se raises also the question of its various functions, namely, of the different types of oath. The oath, in fact, can be divided into two categories: (1) in respect to its nature, and (2) in respect to the law.

In respect to its nature, scholars subdivided the oath into *promissory*, *assertory*, or *declaratory*.[37] The *promissory* oath was one which bound the party, by a religious sanction, to observe a certain course of conduct or to fulfill certain duties in the future, or to demean himself thereafter in a stated manner with reference to specified objects or obligations.[38] Such, for example, was the oath of investiture of any magistrate, or the oath of allegiance to a particular sovereign or government.

The *assertory* oath related to past or present fact or state of facts, as distinguished from the *promissory* oath, which related to future conduct.[39] This oath in turn might be *decisory* or *probative*. The *decisory* oath[40] was taken when one of the parties to a suit, being unable to prove his charge, offered to refer the decision of the case to the oath of his opponent, who was bound either to accept or to tender the same challenge back; otherwise, his refusal was tantamount to a confession. Such an oath was the deciding evidence and constituted the whole trial: proof, judgment, and penalty. It was the same sort of attempt to get the gods to settle a question which we find in the various forms of ordeal. There is no clear evidence as to whether it was actually used before the

36. M. P. Nilsson, *op. cit.*, vol. 1, pp. 54 and 128-29.

37. It seems that, at least until the latter half of the fourth century B.C., the Greeks had not yet incorporated in their legal system a clear distinction between promissory oath and assertory oath, between subjective and objective standards. See R. Hirzel, *Der Eid* (Leipzig, 1902), pp. 10-17; R. J. Bonner and G. Smith, *Administration of Justice from Homer to Aristotle*, 2 vols. (Chicago, 1930-38), vol. 2, p. 146, note 1.

38. H. C. Black, "Oath," *op. cit.*

39. *Ibid.*

40. *Ibid.*

popular courts of Athens. When this oath was taken by the accused, it was known as "exculpatory" or "expurgatory." As indicated, such an oath was administered by a challenge (*proklesis eis horkon*). The *probative* oath was one which confirmed the truth of a statement or testimony; it was only a means of evidence before the dicasts and the assembly of Athens. Such, for example, was the disclaimer oath (*exomosia*).

The *declaratory* oath was a solemn declaration of a claim, made by each litigant before the magistrate. By this oath, the parties agreed not to change the object of debate, not only that each be committed to the other, and both to the judge, but also that the judge be committed to them. It is analogous to the *litis contestatio* (joinder of issue) of Roman law.[41] Such, for instance, were the *diomosia* and *antomosia* in the judicial preliminary hearings; thereby each party was bound to present in advance the facts of his case and how he intended to act in court.

In respect to the law, the oath might be *necessary, voluntary, official,* and *judicial.*[42] The *necessary* oath was one which was required and formulated by law in public and judicial procedure. The *voluntary* oath was the oath of the witnesses which was not required but was permitted by the law, that is, when the witness wished, he could, of his own accord, corroborate his testimony by oath, or when he was challenged by one of the parties, he could also support it by oath. The *official* oath was the one taken by an official when he assumed charge of his office, whereby he declared that he would faithfully discharge the duties of the same, or whatever else might be required by statute in the particular case. This oath has also been referred to as the oath of investiture. It was always *necessary*. Finally, the *judicial* oath was one taken in some judicial proceedings or in relation to some matter connected with judicial proceedings. It could be *necessary* or *voluntary*.

41. G. Glotz, "Jusjurandum," *Darem.-Saglio*. R. Dareste, B. Haussoullier, and R. Reinach, *Recueil des Inscriptions Juridiques Grecques*, ser. 1-2 (Paris, 1895-1904), no. X.

42. H. C. Black, "Oath," *op. cit.*

TWO

The Use of the Oath in Public Life

In the preceding chapter we saw that religion was not only a psychological and theological, but also a juridical institution in ancient Greece; that is, the state was a political and religious society and consequently embraced the whole life of the citizens. We also mentioned that the relationship between gods and men was essentially ritualistic and contractual, and that the oath was precisely an early form of contract. The theory of the Social Contract is not a modern speculation; ancient Greek political thought had already recognized it as a historical fact. The oath was its manifestation: all the citizens and, especially, the public officials, were required by law to swear allegiance to the laws, constitution, and gods of the state. Indeed, the oath was required in every facet of public life, and it constituted, explicitly, the social agreement of the members of the community, both magistrates and citizens.

Oath of the Citizens. To start with, the legitimacy of a child was affirmed by its enrollment in a phratry, for the phratry was a civic and religious unit which played a vital role in the socio-political life of the polis. In Attica, Cleisthenes' reform deprived the phratry, for state reasons, of its political functions, but it still continued to be guardian of the civic status of the citizens; so, every legitimate or adopted child had to be enrolled in it.

The procedure of enrollment required that the father, supported by two witnesses, present the child to the elders of the phratry and swear that it was his legitimate child. An inscription from the beginning of the fourth century B.C. deals with the regulations of the Athenian phratry of the Demotionidai. It runs thus: "The oath formula to be sworn by the (three?) witnesses at the time of the enrollment of the children in the phratry: 'I swear that the child presented by ——— is his legitimate son, born of his wife, and I swear by Zeus Phratrios that I speak the truth. If my oath is true, may I prosper; if I am a perjurer, may misfortune befall me.' "[1]

There might have been different rules and ceremonies for the enrollment of children in different phratries, but the confirmatory oath that established legitimacy, whether taken by the father alone, or by the witnesses, or by both, seems to have been a universal condition.[2]

When the young Athenian reached his eighteenth year, before entering the two-year military service, he underwent a complete examination (*dokimasia*), namely, on his physical condition and legitimate descent. Thereafter, armed with spear and shield, he took the so-called ephebic oath publicly in the temple of the god Agraulos. Thence he was enrolled in the register of his family *deme*, that is, the administrative political unit of Athens, equivalent to a present-day municipality. The oath is attested by several sources which substantially agree as to its content. The following is a translation of an inscription from the middle of the fourth century B.C.:

> Traditional oath of the Epheboi which they must swear:
>
> 'I will not disgrace these sacred arms, nor will I desert the comrade at whose side I shall be stationed.
>
> 'I will defend our altars and our hearths, and will not leave the country smaller, but greater and better, so far as I am able, single-handed or with the help of all.

1. *Syll.*,[3] 921. H. T. Wade-Gery, *Essays in Greek History* (Oxford, 1958), p. 116.
2. Isaeus, 7, 16-17.

'I will obey those who always rule wisely, the established ordinances, and those which will in the future be wisely established.

'If anyone seek to destroy (them) I will oppose him so far as I am able, by myself or with the help of all.

'I will honor the cults of my fathers.

'Witnesses of these shall be the gods Agraulos, Hestia, Enyo, Enyalios, Ares, Athena the Warrior, Zeus, Thallo, Auxo, Hegemone, Heracles, and the boundaries of my native land, wheat, barley, vines, olive-trees, fig-trees. . . .'[3]

The oath is evidently a military, civic and religious contract; military, because while declaring the weapons sacred, it demands a promise to fight bravely in the defense of altars and hearths, and to add to the country's territory; civic, because it requires obedience to the magistrates and loyalty to the institutions; religious, because it also requires due honor to the ancestral gods.

Every Athenian youth was required to take this oath if he wished to become a citizen, i.e., to enjoy political rights. Through this oath, the young man ceased to belong to the family and became part of the polis. Naturalization of aliens was a rare event and, except in Solon's and Cleisthenes' mass franchise, it was personal and by special approval of the Assembly. The process of naturalization, also, consisted not only in the enrollment of the name in some phratry and *deme*, but also in the taking of an oath of allegiance to the state-gods and constitution, probably similar to the ephebic oath, that is, in the making of an explicit social contract with the adopting community.[4]

Similar ephebic oaths were sworn in almost all other poleis, especially from the end of the fourth century. "Thus, the Epheboi of Drerii," says Dittenberger,[5] "swore, for it was customary in all Greek communities to bind the citizens by oath, when they reached their maturity. But it is still disputed whether they took the oath when they entered the Ephebeia (i.e., the two year military term between the age of 18 and 20) or when they left it."

The development of different constitutions, *politeiai,* (demo-

3. Tod, 204. Lycurgus, *Leocrates,* 76-7. Stobaeus, *Florilegium,* 43, 48. Pollux, 8, 105.

4. Dem. 59, 89. The citizenship oath (ephebic or naturalization) could, therefore, form the basis for prosecution of *asebeia.* Cf. Vinogradoff, *op. cit.,* p. 100.

5. *Syll.,*[3] 527[6]; cf. 360[1] and 526.

cratic, oligarchic, etc.) was doubtless a result of the promulgation of law-codes, and the oath of allegiance to a certain constitution (*politeia*) was a result of a new awareness which identified government with personal interest and ideals.

The ephebic oath may be considered as a pledge to or a contract with the historical continuum of the polis, represented by the state guardian-god (*polieus*) or goddess (*polias*), e.g., Athene-Athens; whereas the oath to the *politeia* was a pledge to or a contract with the government in power. Such an oath seems to have been a universal institution in Greece; its formula was local (*enchorios*) and fixed by law (*nomimos*).

"In every city of Greece," says Xenophon (*Memorabilia* 4, 4, 16), "there is a law which requires that all citizens shall promise under oath to be unanimous and act in concord, and they take this oath everywhere. The object of this, I think, is that . . . they may obey the laws." According to Plutarch (*Lyc.* 29), Lycurgus "exacted an oath from the kings and elders, and afterwards from the citizens, that they would abide by the established politeia and observe it until he should come back; then he set out for Delphi." Similarly, at Athens, "all swore to observe" Solon's new *politeia.*[6]

The question soon arose as to whether the historical life or the *politeia* in power formed the juridical identity of the polis.

In a famous passage from the *Politics* (1276a 9-11), Aristotle analyzes this question of the juridical identity of the polis as follows: "Assuming a single population inhabiting a single territory, shall we say that the state retains its identity as long as the stock of its inhabitants continues to be the same (although old members are always dying and new members are always being born), and shall we thus apply to the state the analogy of rivers and fountains, to which we ascribe a constant identity in spite of the fact that part of their water is always flowing in and part always flowing out? Or must we take a different view, and say that while the population remains the same, for the reason already mentioned, [i.e. that the stock of the inhabitants continues to be the same], the *state* may nonetheless change?" In taking the second view, Aristotle continues: "If a polis is a form of association, and if this form of association is an association of citizens in a polity or constitution, it would seem to follow inevitably that when the constitution suffers a change in kind, and becomes a different constitution, the polis

6. Aristotle, *Const. of Athens,* 7, 1. Plutarch, *Solon,* 25.

will also cease to be the same polis, and will also change its identity. . . . If this is the case, it is obvious that the criterion to which we must look in determining the identity of the state is the criterion of the constitution. [The criterion of stock is irrelevant]: whether the same group of persons inhabits a polis, or a totally different group, we are free to call it the same polis, or a different polis. . . . It is a different question, and another matter, whether it is right or wrong for a state to repudiate public obligations when it changes its constitution into another form."[7]

According to Aristotle, therefore, the *politeia* in power, not the historical life of the polis, formed the juridical identity of the state, because only the constitution in power was the legal manifestation of the will of the citizen body by direct representation. Consequently, the polis was the living Athenians, or Corinthians, or Thebans, and the constitution in power was an oath-bound agreement, a social contract among the citizens. "We further proclaim," say the Laws to Socrates (Plato, *Crito*, 51d, e), "and give the right to every Athenian that if he does not like us when he has come of age and has seen the ways of the city . . . he may go where he pleases and take his goods with him. . . . But he who has experience of the manner in which we order justice and administer the state, and still remains, has entered into an implied contract that he will do as we command him."[8] And about a quarter of a century later Demosthenes (25, 16) echoed: "Every law is . . . a general agreement of the whole state, and all men in that state must live according to that law." Therefore, according to Socrates (or Plato?) and Demosthenes, every single adult Athenian was bound by contract to the laws of the polis. This view explains, then, why, after a revolution, all new *politeiai* released their citizens from the oath that bound them to the previous *politeia* and swore them to the new one.

However, the political concept—*viz.*, that the constitution in power formed the juridical identity of the polis—was not applied without qualification. The democratic government of Athens in 404 B.C., for instance, assumed the responsibility of paying any debts incurred by the previous *politeia*, i.e., the Thirty.[9] But, ac-

7. Trans. E. Barker.

8. Trans. B. Jowett.

9. Isocrates, 7, 67-8. Lysias, 12, 59-60. Aristotle, *Const. of Athens*, 40. Dem. 20, 11-12. Cf. Pseudo-Xenophon, *Const. of Athens*.

cording to Aristotle (*Politics*, 1276a), the fact remained that most democracies (established after overthrowing an oligarchy or a tyranny) "were reluctant to fulfill public contracts, arguing that such contracts were made by the governing tyrant and not by the state, and [they were] unwilling to meet other obligations of a similar nature."

Greek thought, in fact, convinced of the organic life, necessity, and transcendence of the polis, had theorized the cyclic evolution of the forms of government: from monarchy to tyranny, to aristocracy, to oligarchy, to democracy, to demagoguery, and back to monarchy to begin the cycle anew. These recurring forms were justified by the rooted belief that, beside the forms of government, the polis continued to exist in its meta-empirical life. Athene-Athens kept a historical identity which commanded some right of loyalty,[10] at least until the end of the fourth century B.C., when the secularization of the polis was almost a *fait accompli* and patriotism had become somewhat sterile.

In conclusion, the solution of the problem of identity may be given by the definition of the state, *viz.*, if by state one means a geographical area, then the constitution in power constitutes the juridical identity of the community; if by state one means a political community, then the community (that is, the historical life of the polis) constitutes the juridical identity, regardless of the types of government.

In ancient Greece, then, as we saw above, the citizens were required to take an oath of allegiance to the constitution in power. Each type of constitution, consequently, developed its own oath. In Athens, for instance, the democratic oath, included in a decree after the restoration of democracy in 410 B.C., had this formula:

"If it be in my power, I will slay by word and by deed, by my vote and by my hand, whosoever shall overthrow the democracy at Athens, whosoever shall hold any public office after its suppression, and whosoever shall attempt to become a tyrant or shall help to install a tyrant.

"And if another shall slay such a one, I will deem him to be without sin in the eyes of the gods and powers above, as having slain a public enemy.

"And I will sell all the goods of the slain and will give one half to the slayer, and will withhold nothing from him.

10. Vinogradoff, *op. cit.*, p. 104.

"And if anyone shall lose his life in slaying such a one, or in attempting to slay him, I will show to him and his children the kindness which was shown to Harmodius and Aristogeiton and to their children.

"And all oaths sworn at Athens or in the army or elsewhere for the overthrow of the Athenian democracy I annul and abolish.

"All the Athenians shall take this oath over a sacrifice without blemish, as the law enjoins, before the Dionysia. And they shall pray that he who observes this oath may be blessed abundantly; but that he who observes it not may perish from the earth, both he and his house."[11]

At Itanos in Crete, according to an inscription[12] which probably dates from the end of the fourth century B.C., all citizens swore:

i. not to deliver the city to the enemy, nor the plain, nor the islands, nor the ships, nor any citizen or his property;

ii. not to participate in any plot or conspiracy, but to consider it as a civic duty to denounce such a plot to the archons;

iii. not to vote for distribution of land or abolition of debts;

iv. not to abolish the equality in all things, human and divine, established by the laws;

v. to work for the defense of the state in war and in peace, each according to his own forces.

A similar oath, but one devoted to more democratic principles, was sworn by the citizens of the Chersonese,[13] also toward the end of the fourth century B.C.

In the oligarchic states, the oath was given only to a privileged class of citizens, and the formula was exactly in opposition to that of the democratic party, which, as shown above, proclaimed that against oligarchs and tyrants, all means, even assassination and treason, were good and honorable. According to Aristotle (*Politics* 1310a), the oath-formula of the oligarchs at his time included the following clause: "I will be hostile to the people and will plan whatever evil I can against them." The oligarchs, furthermore, separated the civil oath from the military oath, apparently because many soldiers did not fully qualify as free citizens. Thus,

11. Andocides, 1, 96-8; trans. K. J. Maidment. Cf. Dem. 20, 159 and Lycurgus, *Leocrates*, 127.

12. *Syll.*,[3] 526.

13. *Syll.*,[3] 360.

according to Andocides (1, 98), the Athenian oligarchs bound the soldiers by a separate military oath.

In the states where the monarchy had been a traditional institution, the oath was a mutual oath between the king and the people, whereas the army swore an oath of obedience to the person of the king.

At Sparta, says Xenophon (*Const. of the Laced.* 15, 7), "they exchange oaths monthly, the ephors in behalf of the people, the king himself in his own behalf. And this is the oath on the king's part: 'I will exercise my kingship in accordance with the established laws of the state,' and on the part of the people the oath runs: 'so long as he (who exercises kingship) shall abide by his oath, we will not suffer his kingship to be shaken.' "

The oath of the kings of Sparta would indicate that the kings were not *sine conditione* by hereditary right or by a mystical tie of a religious character, but by approval of the assembly through the ceremony of the oath on both sides. This mutual oath was then the constitutional basis of the Spartan monarchy.

According to Plutarch (*Pyrrhus* 5), in Epirus, too, the king and the people took mutual oaths: the king swore to obey the laws, and the people swore to keep the monarchy as long as the king respected the laws of the state.

In an inscription[14] found at Pergamum, dated about 263 B.C., there are recorded the mutual oaths that bound "in life and death," the king, Eumenes I, and the officers with the mercenary soldiers. This last, evidently, is an example of military oath to the person of the king.

In states ruled by tyrants, the civil oath was separated from the military oath, but they both seem to have been personal oaths of allegiance to the tyrant. The poet Theognis of Megara (823-4) warned his friend not to serve a tyrant, but not to kill him either, after he had bound himself to him by oath: "Do not exalt a tyrant on hopes, urged by desire of gain, nor kill him after you have bound yourself to him by oath."[15]

From the variety of such partisan oaths one is not surprised

14. Michel, 15.

15. An echo of this admonition is to be found in a medieval English writer, John of Salisbury, *Policraticus*, 8, 20: "To kill a tyrant is not merely lawful, but right and just, provided that the slayer is not bound by fealty to the tyrant." Cf. also, 3, 15.

to see that the dominant party was extremely suspicious lest opposing parties might form anti-constitutional organizations bound by oath (*synomosiai*), and that it tried to release the citizens from oaths that bound them to previous regimes or parties.

However, when the parties had come to an agreement after a civil war, in order to establish a durable unity, a new formula of the civil oath was drawn up and administered to both parties. In fact, a civil war was a conflict of the two allegiances; in it each party pretended to support the constitutional oath (*nomimos horkos*) and accused the other of forming a criminal, subversive political party (*synomosia*). The new oath of reconciliation (*homonoia*) was characterized by a clause stipulating reciprocal amnesty.

In Athens, after the overthrow of the Thirty and the restoration of democracy, at the beginning of Euclides' archonship, 403 B.C., a bill of peace on the following terms was passed under oath: "that there be a universal amnesty for past events, covering everybody except the Thirty, the Ten, the Eleven, and those who have been governors of Peiraeus, and that these also be covered by the amnesty if they render account."[16] This oath of amnesty was taken annually by the council, heliasts, and magistrates.

Similar oaths of reconciliation and amnesty were sworn at Thespiae, where, according to Xenophon (*Hellenica*, 5, 4, 55), the Spartan king Agesilaus in 377 B.C. found the citizens in a state of party feud. The pro-Lacedaemonian faction had wanted to put their political opponents to death; he not only refused to sanction their proceedings, but he also strove to hear their differences and bind them over by solemn oath to keep the peace with one another. A decree of amnesty in Mytilene,[17] dated around 324 B.C., also established the restoration of *homonoia* and bound the factions over by solemn oath to mutual forgiveness. Similarly, at Cynaetha in Arcadia,[18] a decree, sanctioned by oath, bound the citizens to reconciliation (*homonoia*).

Occasionally, the whole citizen body was called to take an oath to ratify a new law, or a peace or alliance treaty,[19] or to guarantee public contracts. A detailed inscription[20] about a public

16. Aristotle, *Const. of Athens*, 39, 6. Cf. Andocides, 1, 90-1.
17. Tod, 201.
18. Polybius, 4, 17, 9.
19. Tod, 42 and 88.
20. Dareste, Haussoullier and Reinach, *op. cit.*, no. IX.

contract, dated toward the end of the fourth century, was found at Chalcis. It deals with the conditions to which a certain Chairephanes agrees to drain the swamp of Ptechai near Eretria. The oath of the Eretrians runs as follows: "I swear by Apollo, Leto and Artemis to let Chairephanes enjoy the granted land, on the condition, agreed upon by the city, that he drain the swamp. If anyone wishes to break the contract with Chairephanes, I shall oppose him with all my power, in accordance with the common oath. If I am faithful to my oath, may I prosper; if I am a perjurer, may misfortune befall me." The inscription continues, stating that if a citizen refused to take the oath, or proposed to break the contract, or refused to have his name inscribed on the oath-stele, he would be punished with full or partial loss of political rights (*atimia*), and his property would be consecrated to Artemis.

When citizens took a public oath, the formula and the names of the swearers were inscribed on a stone. Severe penalties were inflicted upon citizens who did not participate. In Chalcis,[21] for instance, the penalty was loss of citizenship (*atimia*) and the confiscation of property. In Eretria,[22] as has been mentioned above, the penalty was *atimia* for not having one's name on the stele, a fine for proposing not to take the oath, and hereditary *atimia* for whoever proposed a motion contrary to the oath taken. Heavy penalties were also inflicted upon magistrates who neglected to administer an obligatory oath to the citizens.

OATH OF GOVERNMENT OFFICIALS. If an ordinary citizen, in order to enjoy the rights of citizenship, had to submit to an oath, then a fortiori the citizen who was to take a government position had to undergo a similar formality. In fact, the confidence inspired by an oath encouraged the Greeks, and for that matter all nations, to impose upon those who were in authority or were invested with a public function the bonds of an oath, in order to make them fulfill their public duties loyally. The Athenians, among whom the legal technicalities had reached a sophisticated perfection, were demanding, above all, in this respect. Rarely was the civil oath of the citizen sufficient, but, as a rule, a special oath of investiture was also administered.

21. Tod, 42, ll. 34-35: "He who does not take the oath shall forfeit his political rights and property, and one tenth of it shall be dedicated to Zeus Olympios."

22. Dareste, Haussoullier, and Reinach, *op. cit.*, no. IX.

The major political organs of the government in Athens were the council, the courts (*Heliae*), and the magistrates. The council was an organ of the sovereign people. According to Aristotle and Plutarch (but not according to some modern scholars) Solon created it and fixed its number at four hundred. Cleisthenes raised it to five hundred and divided it into ten committees of fifty members each, called prytanies, each prytany being elected by and representing one of the ten tribes. He also divided the year into ten periods, and the prytanies, in rotation, took charge of the state agenda for one of these periods. The function of the council was preliminary and in some spheres even executive.

The formula of its oath has not been preserved in its entirety, but from various fragments we can attempt at least a partial reconstruction. The council members swore:

i. to deliberate in their sessions in accordance with the laws (*kata tous nomous bouleusein*),[23] and in the best interests of the commonwealth (*ta beltista bouleusein toi demoi ton Athenaion*);[24]

ii. not to reveal the secret affairs of the state (*aporreta teresai*);[25]

iii. not to imprison any Athenian citizen who offered three sureties taxed in the same class as himself, except any person found guilty of conspiring to betray the city or subvert the democratic government, or any tax farmer, or his surety, or collector being in default;[26]

iv. to investigate the candidates for public office (*dokimasia*).[27]

In 403 B.C., after the reestablishment of the democratic government, a clause of amnesty was added to the formula. It is reported in Andocides (1, 90-1) as follows: "And I will not accept any information or permit any arrest based on past events except in the case of those who fled from Athens."

In regard to the date of the councilmen's oath (*bouleutikos horkos*), Plutarch (*Solon* 25) states that at the time of Solon the council collectively pledged itself by oath to safeguard the laws. According to Aristotle (*Const. of Athens* 22, 2), however, the oath dates from the time of Cleisthenes: "First of all, in the fifth year after this reform, in the archonship of Hermocreon, they imposed for the first time on the Council of Five Hundred the oath they still

23. Xenophon, *Memorabilia*, 1, 1, 18.

24. Dem. 59, 4. Lysias, 31, 2 and 31.

25. Lysias, 31, 31.

26. Dem. 24, 144 and 147. Cf. Andocides, 1, 93; 4, 3.

27. Lysias, 31, 1.

swear at the present time." It may be concluded, however, that the oath should be dated with the institution of the council (*boule*), and if Solon did in fact institute the council of the Four Hundred, then it would be reasonable to accept that he also instituted the councilmen's oath (*bouleutikos horkos*).[28]

Besides the oath of investiture, the councilmen took other oaths because of their office: they ratified with an oath, for instance, treaties of peace and alliance;[29] they also appointed temporary officials, declaring under oath that the appointments were made without favor or bias.

The heliasts on the other hand were the representatives of the people's sovereignty in the judicial sphere, and their decisions were absolute. At the beginning, when Solon first organized them, they merely formed a court of appeal. Later, that is, sometime between Cleisthenes (c. 510 B.C.) and Ephialtes (462-1 B.C.), the heliasts were divided into panels of 501 and 201 members, called dicasteries, presided over by the thesmothetae. Only occasionally did they meet all together. They continued to be courts of appeal, but now they also took on cases of first resort for major charges. They were chosen by a combination of election and lot every year from the citizen body, so that practically all Athenians were virtually heliasts, and all of them at one time or another took the heliastic oath.

The formula of their oath has been preserved more or less in its genuine entirety in Demosthenes' speech against Timocrates. Various reconstructions[30] have been proposed by scholars; the following is one of them, and it is essentially based on Demosthenes (24, 149; 20, 118; 57, 63). It is a mixture of judicial and political obligations:

"I shall give verdict according to the law and decrees of the people of Athens and of the Council of the Five Hundred.

"In cases not foreseen by the laws, I shall judge according to my best judgment, without favor or enmity.

"I shall not vote to establish a tyrant or an oligarchy, and if

28. For a full discussion on the institution of the council (*boule*) see C. Hignett, *op. cit.*, pp. 92-96. Bonner and Smith, *op. cit.*, vol. 1, pp. 158, 189, and 335.

29. Tod, 29 and 42.

30. For a full discussion on the reconstruction of the heliastic oath see Bonner and Smith, *op. cit.*, vol. 2, p. 152f.; J. H. Lipsius, *Das Attische Recht und Rechtsverfahren* (Leipzig, 1915), p. 150 f.

any man try to overthrow the Athenian democracy, or make any speech or any proposal in contravention thereof, I shall not comply.

"I shall not consent to the cancellation of private debts, nor to the redistribution of lands and houses belonging to the Athenian citizens.

"I shall not restore exiles or persons under sentence of death.

"I shall not expel, nor suffer another to expel, persons here resident, in contravention of the statutes and decrees of the Athenian people or of the council.

"I shall not approve the appointment to any office of any person still subject to audit in respect of another office, to wit: the offices of the nine archons, or of the recorder, or any other office for which a ballot is taken on the same day as for the nine archons, or the office of marshall, or ambassador, or member of the allied congress.

"I shall not suffer the same man to hold the same office twice, or two offices in the same year.

"I shall not take bribes in respect of my judicial action, nor shall any other person, man or woman, accept bribes for me with my knowledge, by any subterfuge or trick whatsoever.

"I am not less than thirty years old.

"I shall give impartial hearing to prosecutor and defendant alike, and shall give my verdict strictly on the charge named in the prosecution.

"I swear by Zeus, Poseidon, and Demeter.

"If I transgress this oath, may destruction fall upon myself, my family and property. If I am faithful to my oath, may I prosper."

After the battle of Munychia in 403 B.C., this oath was expanded and, according to Andocides (1, 91), included at least the following clause of amnesty: "I will harbor no grievances and submit to no influences, but will give my verdict in accordance with the laws in force at the present time."

The oath was taken when the judges entered on their office term. It was promissory and, therefore, a contract, that is to say that if, on the one hand, they were given the right to pronounce judgment upon the life and property of their fellow men, on the other hand, they had to bind themselves, by a dreadful oath, to use this great power according to the laws and to their most just opinion. The curse-formula of this oath was the most solemn of those used, *viz.*, the destruction of oneself, one's clan, and household (*diomosia*: *kat' exoleias autou kai genous kai oikias).*

Practically all orations included an appeal to this oath. The orators did not refrain from stretching its meaning and playing one clause against another. The heliasts were asked in the oath to vote according to the law, and, concerning things about which there were no laws, to decide according to their best judgment. Apparently, this clause of the oath implied a conflict between the law and judgment, which orators and rhetoricians seized upon and exploited to their own ends.

Aristotle, for example, taught in the *Rhetoric* (1, 15f) that this oath could be used as follows: if the law is against one's case, then one must appeal to universal law and equity as more in accordance with justice, i.e., to the oath's clause—"I shall judge according to my best judgment"—which means that the judge should not simply follow the letter of the written laws. On the other hand, if the law is in favor of one's case, one can argue that the clause of the oath—"according to my best judgment"—does not justify the judges in giving a verdict that is contrary to the law, but does save them from the guilt of perjury, should they misunderstand the true meaning of the law.

This clause, furthermore, gave the heliasts a wide range of freedom in cases of unconstitutional laws (*graphe paranomon*). Acting as legislators (*nomothetai*),[31] their verdict could control legislation and annul laws. Thus, they acted as a check on the demagogues and on the Ecclesia. It was their privilege in fact to decide whether a law or their judgment should prevail in cases where these two were at variance. Whatever course they took in each case, they felt they would not be perjurers. The oath was an ideal formula to secure justice rather than a strict set of rules.[32]

The origin of the heliastic oath is connected with the institution of the *Heliae,* and should be dated from the time of Solon, supposing that Solon instituted the *Heliae*. However, the individual

31. The *nomothetai* were a judicial commission consisting of 600 members, selected from among the sworn heliasts. It appears that the oath was the reason why the revision of the laws was entrusted to them rather than to the assembly. Since the assembly was not under oath, it was regarded as less responsible.

32. J. F. Cronin, *op. cit.*

clauses of the formula, as mentioned above, remain controversial matter.

Besides the oath of investiture, the dicasts, that is, heliasts, occasionally swore other oaths on account of their public office. The heliasts, in fact, were not concerned merely with judicial jurisdiction, but also with political obligation. In 446-5 B.C., for instance, they swore to respect the rights of the Chalcideans,[33] agreed upon in the treaty.

We come now to the oath of the third political organ in Athens, the magistrates. Their oath was thought to be a precaution against treason in state officials. In Athens, the newly elected officers were first investigated by the council and then again by the thesmothetai, who gave the final decision as to the qualification of the various candidates; then each official designate had to take the oath of investiture in order to ensure that he would fulfill his state function diligently.

According to Aristotle (*Const. of Athens* 55), after the investigation of qualifications (*dokimasia*),[34] the elected officers went to the *agora*, to a stone consecrated for this purpose, on which the victims were cut up for sacrifices; then, mounting this stone, they swore:

i. that they would govern justly and according to the laws;

ii. that they would not take gifts because of their office;

iii. that if they should take anything, they would set up a golden statue.

After taking the oath, they went from the stone to the Acropolis, took the same oath there and then entered their office.

The magistrates, however, did not have to take any oath at the end of their term of office (*ejuratio*). Such an oath seems to have been peculiar to Rome. But they still had to give an account of their public activity, and their report was checked by other state officials, i.e., the auditors (*logistai*).

The origin of the investiture-oath of the magistrate cannot be determined. Most probably, it antedates the use of money. According to G. Glotz,[35] the archons were bound by the oath of investiture to offer to the gods a statue of gold as penalty if they

33. Tod, 29 and 42.

34. For the oath of the strategoi see Lysias, 9, 15; Plutarch, *Pericles*, 30.

35. G. Glotz and R. Cohen, *Histoire Grecque*, 4th ed., 2 vols. (Paris, 1948), vol. 1, p. 398, note 91.

accepted gifts on account of their administration. The statue had to be *isometretos*. Th. Bergk claims that this word meant that the fine had to be of the same weight in gold as the silver illegally received, but since at this time the ratio of gold to silver was 10:1, the fine had to be tenfold. But *metron* could not have had the meaning of weight; it certainly referred to measure. Consequently, *isometretos* could not mean anything else but that the statue had to be of the same height as the guilty party. This was because the oath goes back to the age when money was not yet in use. The guilty official had to ransom his person, but with such a price that in fact he became insolvent and, consequently, suffered the sentence of total confiscation of property and loss of citizenship (*atimia*), thus becoming an outcast. Whatever the truth, sums up Glotz, the oath of the archons was very old.

In trying to determine the origin of the archonship, Aristotle (*Const. of Athens* 3, 3) says, "They offer as evidence the fact that the nine archons swear to perform their oaths 'as under Acastus,' which seems to indicate that under his rule the descendants of Codrus gave up the kingship in return for the prerogatives given to the archon." Apparently this would indicate that the custom of the oath was as ancient as the institution of the archonship.

As we have already said, the obligation to take the oath before assuming office was extended to all officials, including the magistrates of the *demes*. A decree from Myrrhinus has a résumé of the oath-formula of such local officers:

> The public investigators (*euthynoi*) swore: "I shall not accept any gift, neither myself, nor somebody else, man or woman, on my behalf, in any way or under any pretext whatsoever. If it appears to me that the account is false, I will go over it and calculate the amount of the error."
>
> The auditors (*logistai*) swore: "I shall verify conscientiously the amount of the expenses."
>
> The advocates (*synegoroi*) swore: "I shall support the interests of the deme with justice and shall vote justly."[36]

Finally, an ordinary citizen, charged by the *deme* to undertake an accusation, swore that he had not received, nor would receive, any gifts.

36. G. Glotz, "Jusjurandum," *Darem.-Saglio.*

In international institutions, also, the national representatives were required to take an oath of loyalty to the charter of the institution which they were serving. An inscription,[37] found at Delphi and dated around 380 B.C., for example, gives the oath of the representatives—called *Hieromnemoi*—of the Delphic amphictyony. The formula is in a fragmentary state and, like that of the Athenian dicasts, prescribes a combination of judicial and political functions:

"I shall give the most just verdict possible where there are written laws; where there are no written laws applicable to the case I shall give a verdict according to my own best judgment. I shall never accept a bribe as a dicast nor shall another accept one for me. I shall to the extent of my power exact adjudged penalties. I shall appropriate none of the amphictyonic moneys for my own use nor shall I permit another to appropriate any of the common funds. Thus do I promise by Pythian Appollo and Leto and Artemis. If I swear a good oath I ask that they grant me many blessings, but if I swear a false oath I ask that they give me evils instead of blessings."

The magistrates, like the councilmen and heliasts, from time to time had to take, besides the oath of office, certain other oaths. They had, for instance, to ratify treaties of peace and alliance by oath.[38]

DISCLAIMER OATHS, I.E. THE *Exomosia* AND THE *Antidosis*. Just as a citizen elected to public office had to take an oath before he entered on it, so, too, he had to refuse a public demand or offer by an oath (*exomosia*) before the assembly. In the speech *On the Embassy* (122), Demosthenes refused the appointment as a member of the delegation to Philip on an affidavit. Apparently, the reason for the refusal seemed frivolous to some of the assembly, but the *exomosia* made it final. Similarly, Aeschines (2, 94) also declined the appointment for the same embassy and pleaded illness, which was confirmed by the *exomosia* of his brother and of his physician. But within five or six days, says Demosthenes (19, 124), Aeschines forgot that he was ill, forgot that his brother and physician had sworn the *exomosia* for him, and off he went to see Philip, ignoring

37. *Syll.*,[3] 145. Trans. Bonner and Smith, "Administration of Justice in the Delphic Amphictyony," *CP*, 38 (1943).

38. Thucydides, 5, 47, 9.

all obstacles. Evidently, there was no legal danger for him in ignoring the *exomosia,* except the vengeance of the gods.

According to Aristotle (*Const. of Athens* 49, 2) the council (*boule*) could even grant a discharge from cavalry service to anyone who claimed exemption, under oath, on the grounds of bodily incapacity or lack of means. In oligarchic states, says Aristotle (*Politics* 1297a), "those who possess a property qualification are not allowed to decline offices on oath, but the poor are allowed to do so." Apparently, the poor could also claim tax exemption through the *exomosia.*[39]

Another aspect of the *exomosia* was the *antidosis.* By it the individual citizen gained the right to transfer the tax to another citizen by offering to exchange property with him. A citizen could challenge another on the ground that he was richer than himself and ought to be on the roll of the *leitourgia* (public duty at one's own expense) since the division of burdens should be proportionate to wealth. Accordingly, at the preliminary hearing, each of the two parties had to swear a promissory oath that he would render an accurate inventory of his property within three days. When the account was presented, the party had to swear that it was true and accurate, and had to confirm it by a confirmatory oath.[40]

39. A. H. Jones, *The Athens of Demosthenes* (Cambridge, Eng., 1952), pp. 4-5: "If successive levies come to a total of say a twentieth . . . of their capital, men of the poorest class could claim exemption, while men of the richest class would go on paying till a fifth of their capital was exhausted."

40. Isocrates, 15. Dem. 42.

THREE

The Use of the Oath in Judicial Life

THE OATH OF THE JUDGES. Among the Greeks, the administration of justice in questions of life and property was essentially beyond human jurisdiction, and the right of chosen people to practice it was therefore considered to be a divine concession. In the *Iliad* (9, 98-9) Homer said:

Ζεὺς ἐγγυάλιξεν
σκῆπτρόν τ'ἠδὲ θέμιστας, ἵνα σφίσι βουλεύηισθα.

(Zeus has given you the sceptre and the divine decrees that you may take counsel over the people.)

The oath was believed to guarantee this concession against any abuse. In the *Works and Days* (219) Hesiod declared:

αὐτίκα γὰρ τρέχει Ὅρκος ἅμα σκολιῆισι δίκηισιν.

(For the god Oath keeps pace with wrong judgments.)

And around the middle of the fifth century Aeschylus proclaimed the divine institution of the court of Areopagus. In the *Eumenides* (470-71) Athene said:

> τὸ πρᾶγμα μεῖζον ἤ τις οἴεται τόδε
> βροτοῖς δικάζειν.
>
> (The issue is too big for any mortal man who thinks he can judge it.)

But she quickly added (482-84):

> ἐπεὶ δὲ πρᾶγμα δεῦρ' ἐπέσκηψεν τόδε,
> φόνων δικαστὰς ὁρκίων αἰδουμένους
> θεσμόν, τὸν εἰς ἅπαντ' ἐγὼ θήσω χρόνον.
>
> (since the issue of the case has been appealed here to me, I shall appoint judges of manslaughter and swear them in, and establish a court unto all time to come.)

Gaius[1] seems to echo this belief when he says that the oath came as an effective remedy in settling disputes. "The oath," commented Perrot,[2] "this solemn and religious act, which established a closer rapport between man and God, was necessary to create the judge, to separate him from the people and raise him above them, to give him prestige, to force those whom his decisions would render malcontent to submit to them with unwilling respect."

The practice of swearing the judges or arbitrators was believed to be very old. Plato (*Critias* 119E) says that in Atlantis the old kings used to assemble in the court of justice and there take an oath on a table that bore, besides the laws, also the formula of an oath. According to Aristotle (*Politics* 1285b), in heroic monarchies, the kings, when acting as judges, were sometimes sworn: "Sometimes they judged upon oath, and sometimes without; the form of the oath, when they took one, was the lifting of their scepter." From this one may infer that the kings gave their decisions under oath only when attempts at compromise had failed. Evidently this oath was limited, i.e., restricted to the case in hand and taken only at the request of the litigants. Similar procedure was most probably used also by the elders, when they sat as arbitrators.

The promulgation of the law-codes brought about the formal separation of the administration of justice from the functions of the political magistrates and, thereby, the institution of colleges of

1. *Dig.*, "De Jurejurando," 12, 2.

2. G. Perrot, *Essais sur le Droit Public et Privé de la République Athénienne* (Paris, 1867), pp. 293-94.

judges. Hence, the judicial oath was distinguished from the official oath.[3] Bonner and Smith[4] remarked apropos: "The judicial oath has a higher meaning. The judge is asking for divine aid in making his decision in case there is not enough evidence to make the matter clear otherwise."

The code of Gortyn is one of the most important sources of Hellenic legal procedure. It is generally dated about the first half of the fifth century B.C., but it incorporates many archaic legal principles. According to M. N. Tod,[5] it is "the result of a revision, more or less thorough and systematic, of earlier laws by the Gortynian legislative body, in which some important questions are dealt with only cursorily, while others are wholly neglected. Its significance lies in its realization of a series of new ideas, which raise law to a higher level than before; but it contains references to previously existing law, the knowledge and practice of which is assumed throughout."

The judicial procedure in the Gortynian law was oral; the only proofs admitted were testimony and oaths. In regard to the judgment, there was an important distinction as to whether the judge simply gave judgment (*dikadden*) or decided under oath (*omnynta krinen*): "The judge, in matters in which it has been written that he shall give judgment (*dikadden*) according to witness and oath, shall give judgment (*dikadden*) as has been written, but in other matters he shall take an oath and decide (*omnynta krinen*) according to the pleadings."[6] J. W. Headlam[7] thinks that this distinction between *dikadden* and *omnynta krinen* corresponded to the Athenian distinction between *anakrisis* and *krisis*, and to the Roman distinction between *in iure* and *in iudicio*. However, in the Cretan procedure both parts took place before the same person (*dikastes*).

The judge gave sentence (*dikadde*) whenever he was compelled to pronounce a decision legally determined by the testimony of the witnesses or by the purgatory oath of the defendants. In cases in which there was a *krisis*, that is, in which there were no witnesses and the law did not authorize proof by oath, the judge

3. E. Ziebarth, "Eid," *RE*.

4. Bonner and Smith, *op. cit.*, vol. 2, p. 152, note 6.

5. Tod, 36.

6. *Law of Gortyn*, XI, 26-30.

7. J. W. Headlam, "The Procedure of the Gortynian Inscription," *JHS*, 13 (1892-93), 48-69.

then decided according to his own opinion after listening to both parties and, to guarantee his impartiality, he had to take an oath on his decision (*omnynta krinen*). The following references may serve to illustrate such *kriseis*, in which the judge had to decide under oath:

i. in evaluating a delay;[8]

ii. in evaluating a ransom;[9]

iii. in deciding if a property was inheritable by the heiress;[10]

iv. in deciding if a separation was caused by the husband or the wife;[11]

v. in deciding if a third person had assisted the divorced wife to take objects belonging to her ex-husband;[12]

vi. in regulating a division of property;[13]

vii. in deciding the ownership of a slave.[14]

In Athens Draco is believed to have started the codification of the laws, but Solon apparently completed it and gave it a definite framework, within which the later developments were carried out.

According to the Athenian legal procedure, then, the magistrates in general received all cases and made the inquiry; they referred the important cases to the standing courts of law, but kept for themselves cases of minor charges: the Thesmothetae, says Aristotle (*Const. of Athens* 3, 5), "were then supreme and empowered to give final judgments, and not, like now, only to hold preliminary hearings." There is no question about the fact that they took an oath of investiture when they entered on their office, but there is no certainty as to whether they took a judicial oath every time they handled these minor cases. Since their decisions could be appealed to a jury court, then we might assume that they took no judicial oath, but, if they did, the oath must have been a general promissory one.

Between the end of the fifth century and the beginning of the fourth century, Athens carried out a complete revision of its legal system and one of its results was the creation of public arbitrators.

8. *Law of Gortyn*, I, 10-11. Cf. I, 37-8.
9. *Law of Gortyn*, VI, 51-55.
10. *Law of Gortyn*, IX, 18-22.
11. *Law of Gortyn*, II, 54-55.
12. *Law of Gortyn*, III, 12-16.
13. *Law of Gortyn*, V, 40-45.
14. *Law of Gortyn*, I, 20-23.

These were state officials chosen by lot from the citizen body over sixty years of age. They stood between the magistrates and the judges proper, and handled practically all civil cases of first resort, but their decisions were not final, and litigants could appeal to the court of the heliasts. In order to facilitate such appeals against the decisions of arbitrators, written evidence came into general use about 390 B.C., more than a decade after the institution of public arbitrators.[15] Their function, according to Aristotle (*Const. of Athens* 53), was first of all to effect a compromise. If such attempts failed, then they gave sentence. However, before giving judgment, they had to take an oath on the "sacred stone" in the agora: "the archons," says Aristotle (*Const. of Athens* 55, 5), "go to the stone on which are the victims, cut up for the sacrifices, the same stone on which the public arbitrators take their oath before pronouncing their decisions." There is some question as to whether the oath was taken before the proceedings opened or after (but before the verdict). Bonner and Smith[16] are inclined to believe that the oath was taken before the proceedings opened and that, consequently, it was simply promissory. This view may be corroborated by the fact that the decisions of the public arbitrators could be appealed to the *Heliae*, as mentioned above.

Private arbitrators,[17] however, were an old institution and were chosen by the litigants themselves. Analyzing the cases of arbitration found in the orators, we learn that the private arbitrators also had two functions, to conciliate (*diallattein*) and to judge (*diaitan*).

In the former case, that of conciliation, the arbitrator did not take the oath, because his decision was based substantially on the agreement reached by the parties, which, in turn, was based on their common interest (*kata ta sympheronta*). The content of the judgment here was not given by the opinion of the arbitrator, but by the mutual concessions of the parties.

In the latter case, that of judgment, when large sums were at stake, the arbitrator usually was requested by the parties to take the oath in order to ensure that the verdict which he was about to give corresponded to what appeared to his conscience to be just

15. G. M. Calhoun, "Oral and Written Pleading in Athenian Court," *TAPA*, 50 (1919), 177.

16. Bonner and Smith, *op. cit.*, vol. 2, p. 156.

17. R. J. Bonner, "The Institution of Athenian Arbitrators," *CP*, 11 (1916), p. 191. Bonner and Smith, *op. cit.*, vol. 1, p. 346.

(*dikaion*).[18] The sentence here represented the opinion of the arbitrator, regardless of whether or not it pleased the parties. The oath formula made the decision legally binding. In one case, reported by Demosthenes (29, 58), the private arbitrators said that if they decided on oath, they would condemn the defendant. On hearing this, the defendant refused to allow them to take the oath and went to the public arbitrator instead, whose decision was not final.

In conclusion, there was an essential difference between the function of the conciliatory arbitrator and that of the judicial arbitrator, that is, while the sentence of the sworn arbitrator had juridical force, that of the conciliator had none; and the basis of the difference between conciliation (*diallage*) and judgment (*diaita*) was the oath.

From the orators it also appears that the private arbitrators were reluctant to take the oath and tried to suggest a compromise (*diallage*) that was not legally binding.[19]

But it was not always possible for the arbitrator to carry out his two functions, to reconcile (*diallattein*) and to judge according to the best of his knowledge (*gignoskein*). Sometimes, failing to achieve a conciliation, the arbitrator was not able to know (*gignoskein*) the truth either. In this case, he could not judge according to what was just (*kata to dikaion*), because he did not know the truth; and he could not judge according to the best interest of the parties (*kata to sympheron*), because the parties refused to reach an agreement. There was no alternative but to send the case to the *Heliae*.

The judges proper formed three outstanding courts in Athens: the *Heliae*, the *Ephetai*, and the *Areopagus*. The functions of the *Heliae* have been discussed in Chapter Two. It suffices here to recall that the jurisdiction of the heliasts extended over both public cases and private cases. They were divided into panels (*dikasteria*). In public (criminal) cases, the normal number of a panel was 501; in private (civil) cases, the number was 201. Occasionally larger panels were recruited for extraordinary cases. The Ephetai covered cases of justified and accidental murder (*phonos akousios*). Sometime in the fourth century B.C., however, their jurisdiction was absorbed by the heliasts. The Aeropagus dealt with premeditated

18. Isaeus, 2, 30-33.
19. Dem. 52, 30-31.

murder, assault with intent to murder and arson. Its judicial oath was its oath of investiture; it was permanent and did not have to be renewed every time it sat in tribunal. Information as to the precise nature of the oaths for the *Areopagus* and the *Ephetai* is practically non-existent, but their decisions were final.

Everywhere in Greece the exercise of judicial function was subordinated to the condition of the oath. According to Isocrates (19, 15), the judges of Aegina swore "to vote in accordance with the laws." When the assembly of 883 members in Eresos set up as a court to pass judgment on the tyrants, it took the following oath: "I shall judge in this case, in matters dealt with by the laws, according to the laws; in matters not foreseen by the laws, I shall try to decide as justly as possible. If I condemn, I shall decide the penalty by a just estimate. I shall swear by Zeus and Helios."[20]

The well-known inscription[21] from Cnidus, dealing with an international dispute between Cos and Calymna, runs thus:

"The *strategoi* (generals) shall administer the oath to the judges called to the trial. . . . The oath shall be the following:

" 'I swear by Zeus, Apollo Lykeion and Earth, that I shall judge about the things which the litigants have presented under oath according to what might appear most just. I shall not judge according to a witness, if this witness seems to me not to have been telling the truth. I have not received any gifts in regard to this process, myself, or another—man or woman—for me, in any way or by any subterfuge whatsoever.

" 'May I prosper, if I keep my oath, but may misfortune befall me, if I am a perjurer.' "

Like court judges, the judges of any form of contest, such as literary and athletic contests, had to take promissory oaths before they set out to judge.[22] The oath sworn by the judges at Olympia, before the opening of the games, is well known. In the presence of the contestants, over the flesh of a boar, they swore by Zeus Herkeios to vote "with justice and without accepting gifts."[23]

The principle of the judicial oaths seems to have been expressed very clearly in a law at Delphi: "Let it be law that they

20. *Syll.*,[3] 953[2]. Cf. Dareste, Haussoullier, and Reinach, *op.cit.*, no. XXVII.

21. *Syll.*,[3] 953. Cf. Dareste, Haussoullier, and Reinach, *op. cit.*, no. X.

22. Andocides, 4, 21. Dem. 21, 17, 65.

23. Pausanias, 5, 24, 9-10.

judge under oath" (*hoti de ka houtoi krinonti omosantes, touto kyrion esto*).[24]

Throughout Greece, therefore, every person called upon to judge (*krinein*) was subject to the condition of an oath; the oath was required to give the decisions coercive, executive force. It was perhaps this prerequisite oath that caused the judges sometimes to be called "the sworn people" (*epomotai*) or (*horkomotai*).[25]

In conclusion there were two types of oaths for judges: promissory and assertory. The promissory oath was taken before the proceedings opened and its formula would probably include the following clauses:

i. to listen impartially to both sides;

ii. to judge according to the laws;

iii. to accept no gifts, either personally or through any third party, because of the office;

iv. to vote without favor or enmity, but according to justice.

The assertory oath was taken after the proceedings had taken place, and it guaranteed the impartiality of the judge, i.e., the justice of his decision.

In certain cases, the promissory oath was judicio-political; these would be the cases in which the judges had certain legislative powers, as did the heliasts of Athens.

THE OATH OF THE LITIGANTS. In the early times of society the litigants were also the judges of their own disputes, with their relatives as both co-judges and helpers. There was no public justice as yet; the king or the local lord, only when invited, sat as an arbitrator. In this early age, the principle of an eye for an eye and a tooth for a tooth—the *lex talionis*—was the only law accepted. Blood was washed away by blood. The dead man's spirit haunted his relatives and clamored for vengeance. This was essentially an era of self-help and reprisals.

But alongside the custom of self-help and reprisals, there developed, as soon as people began to settle down, the custom of divine arbitration. The divine will was believed to manifest itself in duels, ordeals and oaths.

In the *Iliad*, for example, the duel between Menelaus and

24. G. Glotz, "Jusjurandum," *Darem.-Saglio*.
25. Tod, 34.

Paris (3, 15) and the oath which Menelaus offered to administer to Antilochus after the chariot race (23, 580f) may be considered as illustrations of divine arbitration. Cases of ordeal are encountered even in the fifth century. According to Pausanias (7, 25, 13), the priestesses of the goddess of Earth in Aegira of Achaia could prove their chastity by drinking the blood of a bull. According to Diodorus Siculus (11, 89f), at Palika in Sicily, there was a belief that only the pure and innocent could approach the sulphurous springs, whereas the perjurer would be burned. In Sophocles' *Antigone* (264), the Messenger offered to undergo ordeal by fire and to take a decisory oath in order to prove that his message was true: "We are prepared to hold in our hands red-hot iron, to walk through fire, to swear before the gods that we did not do it, nor shared in the plan when it was plotted and when it was carried out." In Aeschylus' *Eumenides* (429), Orestes, when challenged to take an exculpatory oath to cleanse himself from the charge of matricide, refused the oath through fear of the deity, and instead pleaded justifiable murder.[26]

The exculpatory oath was an ordeal in words, and vice versa, the ordeal was an oath in action. Both left the matter of punishment to the gods. But in the ordeal, the perjurer was believed to be punished on the spot; whereas in the oath, the gods might postpone punishment so that it fell even on the descendants of the perjurer. It is not, therefore, surprising that the members of a primitive society were willing to accept an oath in the name of the gods as final and as constituting a whole trial. The oath was then both proof and judgment without recourse, that is, it was a divine judgment. In fact, proof was not yet distinguished from judgment, nor even from penalty: proof, judgment, and penalty were all one in this embryonic stage of judicial procedure; the arbitrators sat like passive spectators, who witnessed the contest of the litigants. This oath was sometimes referred to in Greece as the oath of Rhadamanthus, a legendary king of Crete. It was believed that he asked both parties to take the oath, assuming that from fear of the gods only the innocent would dare take it.

With the promulgation of the law-codes, however, state justice

26. Dem. 23, 74: "(our legal ancestors) arguing that Orestes, having killed his mother and confessing the fact, was acquitted by the gods acting as judges, they formed the opinion that there is such a thing as justifiable murder, for gods could not have given an unjust verdict."

attained authority enough to formulate judgments and enforce them. Proof and judgment ceased to be one; thereby, the oath, in courts, was accepted only as a proof; outside the courts, however, it preserved its original power.

In the law of Gortyn, the assertory oath of either litigant was still used as the deciding evidence. The oath as such, however, was admitted only in cases expressed by law; these cases, by and large, were those in which the testimonial proof did not exist or was insufficient. The judge then administered the oath to the party prescribed by law; but in cases in which the law did not prescribe which of the litigants was to take the oath, the judge decided which was to be sworn, that is, the *horkioteros*, and according to whether the party accepted or refused the oath, he won or lost the case *ipso facto*.

Generally, the defendant had the advantage of the assertory oath, i.e., he was the one to be sworn (*horkioteros*). For instance, the judge granted the purgatory oath:

i. to a divorced woman who had been accused of taking property belonging to her ex-husband in a *rerum amotarum* suit;[27]

ii. to a merchant who denied that he had any obligation to a partner;[28]

iii. to a judge accused of having delayed beyond the time prescribed by law in giving a decision in a suit.[29]

However, there are, in the law of Gortyn, exceptional cases in which the advantage of the oath was granted to the plaintiff, i.e., the plaintiff was considered to be the *horkioteros*. For instance, the judge would administer the oath:

i. to a slave girl who complained that she had been violated by her master;[30]

ii. to a creditor in a suit to renew the title to a debt on the death of a debtor;[31]

iii. to an offended husband, who, in a reparation suit against the adulterer, claimed that the occasion of the adultery was not a snare set by him;[32]

27. *Law of Gortyn*, III, 5-9. Cf. XI, 46-50.
28. *Law of Gortyn*, IX, 51-54.
29. Dareste, Haussoullier, and Reinach, *op. cit.*, no. XIX B.
30. *Law of Gortyn*, II, 15.
31. *Law of Gortyn*, IX, 35-40.
32. *Law of Gortyn*, II, 36-45.

iv. to an owner of an animal injured or killed by the animal of another person.[33]

The defendant's exculpatory oath was normally by itself sufficient for acquittal, but the plaintiff's assertory oath had usually to be corroborated by oath-helpers.

In Athens, state justice entered its maturity with Solon. Solon,[34] establishing a new judicial court, permitted the oath only when there was no other evidence available and allowed both parties to take it. In cases where both parties took the oath, it was up to the judge to decide who swore rightly (*poteros euorkei*). Consequently, in these instances, the decision rested *de facto,* not on the oaths of the parties, but on the opinion of the judge. Thus, in the Athenian courts also, the oath, having been separated from the judgment, ceased to be the whole trial and became merely probative.

According to Aristotle (*Rhetoric* 1, 15), there were in his time five kinds of proof, *viz.,* laws, witnesses, contracts, tortures and oaths. The oath was the last resort, the *ultimum praesidium* of the parties. It was used as a proof only when all other proofs were lacking, and it was introduced by way of challenge (*proklesis eis horkon*).[35] If the challenge was accepted, the party who administered it phrased the formula and watched carefully to detect any evasion from it.[36] The party who accepted it deposited a sum of money, which he forfeited in case he later refused to fulfill his promise to swear: "After the action was introduced," says Demosthenes (33, 13), "Parmeno tendered an oath to Apaturius about some details of the complaint, and he accepted it, and furthermore made a deposit to be forfeited if he failed to take the oath."

The challenge, therefore, when accepted, amounted to a formal contract about the formalities and the effect of the oath. It designated the official who received the security money, presided over the administration of the oath, and recorded the probative or

33. Dareste, Haussoullier, and Reinach, *op. cit.*, no. XVIII.

34. *Lexica Segueriana*, v. "Doxastai": "Judges are those who determine which one of the litigants swears rightly. For Solon ordains that the defendant, when there are neither contracts nor witnesses, should swear, and the plaintiff in like manner."

35. Cf. Dem. 29, 33, 52, 54; 39, 3; 40, 10; 49, 65; 54, 40; 55, 27. According to Pollux (8, 62): "*Proklesis* is the solution of the trial based on a definite oath, or testimony, or torture, or something similar." See also Suidas, "*Proklesis,*" *Lexicon.*

36. *Iliad*, 23, 580f. Dem. 29, 52; 59, 60.

decisory effect of the oath. If there was no agreement or formal contract about the oath, it had no legal power at all.[37]

If the challenge was rejected, it had no legal power,[38] but the challenger could use the refusal as an argument for his claim. Moreover, such a refusal was liable to create a serious prejudice in the judges and might be considered by them tantamount to a confession.

The striking aspect of these oath challenges, found in the orators, both outside and in the courts, was the fact that the party seldom tendered the oath to his opponent, but rather volunteered to take it himself, or had one of his witnesses volunteer to take it. But, in this case, it was relatively easy for the challenged party to reject the challenge by exposing the dubious character of the challenger;[39] or by a counterchallenge to take the oath himself or have one of his own witnesses volunteer to take it.

As a general rule, oath challenges of this kind were very seldom accepted. Usually, to every challenge there was a counterchallenge, and the result was mutually abusive charges of impiety and atheism, as Demosthenes' speech against Conon (40f) shows: "Surely Conon, a man of this description (i.e. an inveterate perjurer) is not to be believed on his oath. . . . But, a man who . . . if forced to swear, will only take the legal (*nomimos*) oath, imprecating destruction upon himself, his kin and his household (*kat' exoleias autou kai genous kai oikias*), is more to be believed than one who swears by his children or is ready to pass through fire. I then . . . offered to take the oath here cited. . . . 'I swear by all the gods and goddesses that I have suffered from Conon these things about which I am suing him—that I have received blows (from him), that my lip was so cut open that it had to be sewn up, and that I am prosecuting him because I have been outraged by him. If I swear truly, may blessings be mine and may I never be thus injured again; if I am forsworn, may I perish utterly, I and all I possess or ever may possess.' "

And so the plaintiff makes sure that he is not outdone by Conon, the defendant: Conon offered to take the exculpatory oath with impressive curses; the plaintiff refused it, charging Conon

37. Dem. 55, 35; 54, 40: Conon, in fact, could not swear a binding oath, unless his opponent administered it to him.

38. Dem. 29, 54; 49, 65.

39. Dem. 49, 65.

with being an inveterate perjurer and offered instead to take a very solemn oath himself, as a law-abiding and god-fearing man.

In his third speech against Aphobus, Demosthenes was forced to defend one of his witnesses, a certain Phanus, accused of false testimony. The alleged false testimony was Phanus' deposition that Aphobus had admitted, before the public arbitrator, that Milyas was a freedman. In the speech (51f) Demosthenes declared that he would pay Aphobus whatever damage Phanus' deposition caused him, if Aphobus proved his allegations by a solemn oath: "concerning this matter, said I, I will hand over to you [the slave] who has the copies of these things about which you challenged me; and if, after I have sworn that you admitted the man to be free and that you so testified against Damon, you will swear to the contrary with imprecations upon your daughter, I surrender to you all things, which the tortured slave will show that you had first demanded, and the penalty, which you were condemned to pay, shall be reduced by that amount which you demanded of Milyas, in order that you may not sustain injury by the witnesses."

Had Aphobus accepted the challenge, would he have won the case? Was the probative power of such an oath peremptory on the judges? Glotz[40] suggests that *de iure* the judges were not bound by any kind of proofs, including the oath: Solon had freed them from all external evidence and bound them by oath to judge according to their conscience.[41] But the passages (Dem. 54, 40; 55, 35) seem to leave little doubt that if Conon and the defendant in the speech against Callicles had sworn the legal oath (*nominos horkos*) in accordance with the challenge (*proklesis*), then the judges would have been bound to award them the decision. However, there is no instance in any of the orators of a probative oath before a dicastery that was accepted and actually produced the solution of the case (*lysis tes dikes*).

In Demosthenes' speech against Callipus (15f), Apollodorus also implies that, had his father Pasion really been tendered the solemn oath before the arbitrator and refused it, he would have lost the case.

It must, however, be noted here that Apollodorus is referring to a suit not before a dicastery but before a private arbitrator, Lysitheides, who is not an official judge with invested authority,

40. G. Glotz, "Jusjurandum," *Darem.-Saglio.*

41. See note 34 above and the corresponding section in the text.

but a moderator. In cases of arbitration, the rules of procedure were determined, not by law or by the arbitrator, but by the litigants themselves: the arbitrator simply witnessed the agreements and recorded them. If the litigants agreed to solve their dispute by a solemn decisory oath, the arbitrator would give the award on the basis of the oath.

There is only one instance before an arbitrator, in which the oath challenge was accepted and the decision was given on the basis of it. It occurs in Demosthenes' speech against Boiotus II (10f): "After many meetings took place about these things, my father declared that he was not convinced that these fellows [Boiotus and Pamphilus] were his sons; at last, Plangon, men of the jury (for the whole truth shall be told you), having in concert with Menecles laid a snare for my father, and having deceived him by an oath, which all mankind held to be the greatest and most dreadful, agreed that if he paid her thirty minas, she would make her brothers adopt these fellows as sons, and that, on her part, if my father challenged her before an arbitrator to swear that these fellows were really his, she should not accept the challenge. . . . These things being agreed upon . . . . he went to the arbitrator, and Plangon, violating all the agreements, accepted the challenge and swore in the Delphinium an oath directly contrary to her [previous] oath . . . and so my father was forced by his own challenge to submit to the award . . . and introduce them [these fellows] to his clansmen. The defendant he enrolled under the name of Boiotus, and the other under the name of Pamphilus."

In conclusion, the oath challenge could produce the solution of the suit (*lysis tes dikes*) both before the arbitrators and the magistrates in the preliminary hearings (*anakrisis*), but there is no certain evidence that it was also introduced before the dicasts and that, furthermore, it was peremptory on them.[42] The oath chal-

42. R. J. Bonner, *Evidence in Athenian Court* (Chicago, 1905), p. 76, however, thinks that the oath-challenge could be administered also before the dicasts, and gives as reference C. Mederle, *De Jurejurandi in Lite Attica Decem Oratorum Aetate Usu* (Munich, 1902), p. 26: "Ego autem saepius etiam in ipso iudicio esse iuratum arbitror. Quod colligo ex hoc loco Isaei (De Astyph. her. 24):

> δοκεῖ δέ μοι κἄν ὀμόσαι ἄσμενος εἴ τις αὐτῶι
> ὅρκον διδοίη.

Hierocles enim iste et ipse petebat vel a parte petentis stabat. Cum autem deferri ei posset jusjurandum, etiam, ut juraretur, permissum esse concludimus."

lenge could be tendered to both litigants and to their witnesses.

Besides the oath challenges there developed in Athens during the sixth century the declaratory oath, which solemnly attested the sincerity of the litigants' claims before a magistrate in the preliminary hearings.

The plaintiff's oath was called *promosia,* that of the defendant *antomosia,* and the exchange of oaths *amphiorkia,* which, however, in cases of homicide, was more properly referred to as *diomosia.* The *promosia* (from the verb *pro-omnymi*) etymologically meant the oath sworn first. Demosthenes used it only twice (29, 52 and 57), and there is nothing in his speeches (or in other sources, for that matter) which might indicate the degree of solemnity of this oath or to what circumstances it might be restricted. Pollux (8, 55) defined it as follows: "*Promosia* is an oath which the plaintiff swears, [asserting] that the denunciations are true." The *promosia,* therefore, was not a special kind of oath; it simply indicated an oath sworn first in a dispute, and by and large, this was the plaintiff's oath. *Antomosia* etymologically meant an oath that was opposed to that of another party. At first it must have referred only to the defendant's oath (*Isaeus* 3, 6; 5, 4), which was taken in opposition to that of the plaintiff; later, it indicated the oaths which both litigants swore in all cases, except in homicide trials, to attest the sincerity of their declarations.[43] *Amphiorkia* etymologically meant the oath of both parties; but it is found only in Pollux. *Diomosia* etymologically can indicate: (i) both oaths, that of the plaintiff and that of the defendant; this meaning is derived from *dia* in the sense of "between," "among," as in the verb *dialegesthai* (to converse with another); (ii) a great solemn oath; this meaning is derived from *dia* in the sense of "altogether," "thoroughly," as in the verb *diollynai* (to destroy utterly);[44] (iii) a co-oath; in this sense it might have been used at the time when "oath-helpers" were employed, but no longer by the fifth century B.C.[45] However, Demosthenes, for instance, used *diomosia* only with the second meaning, i.e., a great and solemn oath with the following dreadful imprecation:

κατ' ἐξωλείας αὑτοῦ καὶ γένους καὶ οἰκίας

43. *Syll.*,[3] 953[4]. Bonner and Smith, *op. cit.*, vol. 2, p. 162 f.

44. Cf. Dem. 18, 283 and 286; 23, 63-69; 47, 70-73; 49, 20 and 67; 57, 22; 59, 10. Antiphon, 5, 11. C. Mederle, *op. cit.*

45. Cf. G. Glotz, "Jusjurandum," *Darem.-Saglio.*

(to invoke destruction upon oneself, one's kindred and one's own house)

not only in murder cases, but also in other solemn instances.

These introductory oaths were obligatory and, according to Dareste, Haussoullier, and Reinach,[46] and Glotz,[47] formed a procedure which was analogous to the *litis contestatio* (joinder of issue) of Roman law: they determined the object of the debate.

In cases of murder, the plaintiff in his solemn oath had to include the following three conditions:

i. that he was entitled to prosecute, *viz.*, that he stood within the required relationship to the deceased: "for the law, men of the jury, enjoins that the relatives shall prosecute;"[48]

ii. that the defendant was guilty;[49]

iii. that he would confine himself to the actual charge without introducing irrelevant matter.[50]

The defendant swore with the same solemnity (*diomosia*) that he did not commit the murder: "The prosecutor," declares Antiphon (6, 16), "swore that I instigated the murder of Diodotus; whereas I swore that I did not cause his death either by my own hand or by instigation." About a generation later, Lysias (10, 11) said: "The prosecutor swears that the defendant has killed, and the defendant swears that he did not."

In civil cases, both parties merely swore to the truth of their pleadings.

The *amphiorkia* and the *diomosia* were, therefore, not so much evidence for the trial like the oath-challenge as, rather, a contract for a trial. Glotz[51] attempts to explain their origin by the scene on the shield of Achilles in the *Iliad* (18, 499f): the plaintiff declares before the people that he has not received the blood-money. The defendant declares that he paid the blood-money. They agree to bring the dispute to an arbitrator. If the litigants had supplemented their statements with an exchange of oaths, these would have constituted the *antomosia*.

Ziebarth[52] and Bonner and Smith,[53] on the other hand, con-

46. Dareste, Haussoullier, and Reinach, *op. cit.*, no. X.
47. G. Glotz, "Jusjurandum," *Darem.-Saglio.*
48. Dem. 47, 72. Also, 43, 57.
49. Dem. 59, 10.
50. Antiphon, 6, 9. Also, 5, 11.
51. G. Glotz, "Jusjurandum," *Darem.-Saglio.*
52. Ziebarth, "Eid," *RE.*
53. Bonner and Smith, *op. cit.*, vol. 2, p. 161f.

sider the *amphiorkia* and *diomosia* to be developments of Solon's enactment which permitted both parties to take the oath.

In the *Laws* 12 (948D), Plato violently criticizes the Athenian legal custom of administering the oath to both parties on the subject of the dispute. This custom, says Plato, was good in the times of Rhadamanthus, when religion was supreme and everybody deeply believed in the existence of the gods. But as soon as there are some people who affirm that there are no gods, and others are convinced that the gods are not concerned with human affairs; as soon as most people believe that the gods can be bribed with some small offerings or meaningless adulations, and that they can thus earn acquittal from the penalties due to their crimes, then it is necessary that the laws change. The policy followed by Rhadamanthus is no longer practical, because feelings in respect to the gods are no longer the same. The oath should be restricted to those cases in which there is nothing to be gained by perjuring oneself. In all cases in which there is something to gain by denying a fact, only the ordinary means of justice should be permitted.

Why did the Athenian law compel both parties to take the oath? Was this not, in effect, to compel perjury by law? The law that compelled both parties to swear must have taken into consideration the fact that the party oath had merely a declaratory, not a probative force. It was left to the court to decide who swore rightly (*poteros euorkei*) regardless of the intention of the oath-taker;[54] so, a man who unintentionally swore a false oath still perjured himself.[55] It seems that the Athenians failed to make a

54. It appears, then, that the Athenian legislator Solon (cf. "Doxastai" in *Lexica Segueriana*) acted on a different principle from that of Plato's Rhadamanthus, who thought that the defendant, if he were conscious of his guilt, would admit his error and not burden himself and his family with the dreadful curse of the oath. Cf. Bonner and Smith, *op. cit.*, vol. 1, p. 173 f.

55. The formula of the oath acted *ex opere operato,* that is, by the automatic efficacy of the ritual words of the formula. See, for comparison, the procedure of the *legis actiones* in Roman law. B. Nicholas, *An Introduction to Roman Law* (Oxford, 1962), pp. 159-60, makes, for instance, the following comment on the Roman *stipulatio*: "But the validity of a *stipulatio*, like that of any formal act, came from its form and not from the agreement which the form no doubt embodied. For agreement was neither necessary nor sufficient. It was not necessary, and therefore the debtor could not plead that he was mistaken, that his mind did not go with the act; it was not sufficient, and therefore if the form had been defective (e.g. because the debtor said 'promitto' instead of 'spondeo'), the creditor could not plead that there had nevertheless been an agreement in substance." The obligation, therefore, was created not by the

legal distinction between the subjective and objective aspects of the oath,[56] or, perhaps, they simply disregarded the subjective aspect which was considered to be under the jurisdiction of the gods.[57] The will or intention had juridical value only when formally expressed, i.e., when it became an external, objective act, but not when it remained internal, i.e., a subjective act.

According to E. Rohde,[58] such a compulsory oath, taken by both parties to guarantee the justice of their claim, could not in any circumstances serve as proof, since at least one of the parties must have perjured himself. This double oath, then, even though taken with particular solemnity, could not have been regarded as a juridical matter at all; it must have been strictly religious: the oath-taker invoked a dreadful curse upon himself, if he broke his oath, and devoted himself, his kindred, and his household to the curse-goddesses (the *Arai*) or the Furies, who were to avenge in the underworld dead men who had sworn to a falsehood, and to the gods above who were to punish on earth his children and his whole kith and kin. Now, if the perjured party lost the case, he would be punished twice, by the court and by the gods; but, if, by chance, he won the case, the gods would still punish him, for the curse inevitably fulfilled itself. Thus, according to Rohde, the double oath was an added precaution to the judicial inquiry; human punishment might or might not reach the perjurer, but divine punishment would never fail to reach him. Thus, the oath, being an appeal to a higher court, supplemented human justice, or rather—we should say—human justice supplemented the oath-taking, for the oath-taking preceded the state justice.

After the points of a dispute between two litigants had been formulated by the magistrate and the day for trial had been established, it might happen that one of the two litigants could not attend the trial because of illness, travel abroad, military duty in the field, or some other reason. In such a situation, the party concerned sent to the court two or more witnesses who would ex-

voluntas of the parties, but by the formula of the oath; hence, the necessity that whoever administered the oath phrase also the formula of the oath.

56. Cf. V. Ehrenberg, *Aspects of the Ancient World* (New York, 1946), p. 85: "Apparently Solon followed earlier thought in that he did not yet really distinguish between subjective feelings and objective facts."

57. Cf. Tacitus, *Ann.* 1, 73: *Deorum iniurias dis curae.*

58. E. Rohde, *Psyche*, trans. W. B. Hillis (New York, 1925), p. 212, note 156.

plain the reasons for his absence, would support them with a probative dilatory oath (*hypomosia*),[59] and would ask the court for a delay of the proceedings. In the speech against Olympiodorus (25f), for instance, Demosthenes gives military service in the field as a reason for postponement of the trial: "When the archon summoned all the claimants into court according to the law, I entered a sworn statement asking for an adjournment on the ground that the defendant, Olympiodorus, was abroad on a campaign in the public service." In the speech against Theocrines (43f), illness is used as an excuse for adjournment: "When the indictment was introduced, someone entered an affidavit to postpone the proceedings on the ground that Demosthenes was ill."

Against these delays and maneuverings of a party, the opponent could counteract by an anti-delay or anti-adjournment affidavit, called *anthypomosia*, proving by oath that the cause for stay was insufficient or purposely created in order to thwart justice: "But against this affidavit of delay (*hypomothentos de toutou*)," continues Demosthenes (48, 25), "our opponents made a counter-affidavit (*anthypomosanto*), accusing Olympiodorus of being absent on account of the trial and not on account of public service."

If a litigant failed to attend the trial on the appointed day without showing cause, he lost the case by default; however, he could have the judgment suspended if he put in an affidavit (*hypomosia*) within the time prescribed by law, giving a reasonable excuse for his absence and showing sufficient cause that the case should be reheard. In the speech against Midias (81ff), Demosthenes reminds the dicasts that the case had already been brought before an arbitrator, a certain Strato of Phalerum, and that Midias failed to attend without due cause and, consequently, lost the case by default. After the arbitrator gave the decision, Midias tried to have the case reopened, but refused to take the dilatory oath (*hypomosia*) to prove the reasons for his absence before the arbitrator. So the arbitrator's judgment automatically became absolute and final.

Another instance in which the dilatory oath was used was in a case of unconstitutional law (*graphe paranomon*). Any Athenian citizen had the legal right to indict a bill within a year after its passage as illegal and unconstitutional. He gave notice of his

59. *Lexicographi Graeci*, v. "Hypomosia" and "Anthypomosia."

intention to indict the bill by a public declaration supported by oath. According to Demosthenes (18, 103), this oath had the effect of suspending the enforcement of the decree until the unconstitutionality of the bill could be tried.

From these instances it is clear that the dilatory oath (*hypomosia*) had probative force. It was not a mere formality, but constituted sufficient cause to produce a stay of execution of a sentence, a legal adjournment, and a stay of enforcement of a decree.

The Attic orators sometimes speak of oaths taken after judgment has been passed. In the speech on the estate of Menecles (32f and 38f) Isaeus reports that the arbitrator, after having given his decision, compelled the litigants to swear that they would render service to each other in the future, according to the ability of their means, in word and deed.

At the time of Aeschines (2, 87-8), the party who won the case in a homicide court had to cut in pieces a sacrificial victim and take a solemn oath on it, affirming that those of the dicasts who had voted on his side had voted what was true and right, and that he himself had spoken no falsehood. He then called down destruction on himself and his household if this were not true and prayed for many blessings on the jurors.

Similar legal procedures seem to have been customary throughout Greece. In a fifth century (460-55 B.C.) inscription[60] from Halicarnassus, for instance, the exiles, returned as a result of an amnesty, were granted an eighteen month delay to vindicate any real estate. During this delay, all assumptions were in their favor. The judges would grant the decisions in favor of the plaintiff if he stated his claim under oath and the recorders (*mnemones*) corroborated it by a deposition on oath. But, after the expiration of these eighteen months, the occupier *de facto* of the contested property was given the advantage of the decisory oath, which he had to take in the presence of the claimant.

According to a law of the Labyadai at Delphi, any member of the phratry who contested the validity of a fine was acquitted if he justified his case by a solemn oath: "after he had legally sworn, let him be acquitted" (*exomosas ton nomimon horkon, lelystho*).[61] Similarly, we are told by Thucydides (5, 77) that when

60. Tod, 25. *Syll.*,[3] 45.

61. Schwyzer, E. *Dialectorum Graecarum Exempla Epigraphica Potiora* (Leipzig, 1923), no. 323D.

the Argives demanded from the Epidaurians the offering of a sacrifice which the latter did not believe was due, the Lacedaemonians proposed to settle the dispute by administering the decisory oath to the Epidaurians, and should they refuse, it would be administered to the Argives instead.

As to the declaratory oaths (*amphiorkia* and *diomosia*) in the preliminary investigation, Plutarch,[62] for example, reports that at Sparta, an arbitrator, chosen by two opponents, imposed an oath on them before he started the proceedings. The inscription[63] from Cnidus about the arbitration between Cos and Calymna also implies that the parties took oaths before the proceedings opened. Furthermore, the definition of *antomosia*, given by Harpocration, seems to imply that the preliminary oaths were common throughout Greece.

THE OATH OF THE WITNESSES. In primitive customs, the relatives joined the parties in cases of dispute. After the custom of private war had passed into disuse, but before the recognition of disinterested deposition, there was a period when the members of the clan and phratry mutually supported each other before the tribunals.

In this period of transition, the witnesses, i.e., the relatives and friends, took joint oaths with the principal. The oath of the witnesses and that of the party were seldom separated, because the witnesses declared themselves for one party or the other; they were sworn partisans. According to Bonner and Smith[64] the word *arogoi* in the *Iliad* (18, 502 and 23, 574), for instance, "has such a definite partisan significance that it is not going too far to say that the psychology back of the Homeric scenes is the same as that behind compurgation." The oath-helpers, then, were partisans in the sense that they intended to support the principal by force, if need be. The feuds were not personal, but familial, that is, the family through its chief either surrendered or demanded the alleged culprit; either offered or demanded a compensation for a wrong done; or, lastly, prepared for reprisal.

Apparently, the witnesses did not make a deposition of what they knew; they simply took an oath as evidence of the truthfulness

62. Plutarch, *Apophth. Laced. Arch.*, p. 218D.
63. *Syll.*,[3] 953.
64. Bonner and Smith, *op. cit.*, vol. 2, p. 189.

of the principal's oath. There was no way of evaluating such witnesses, except by counting the number of the oaths: the party who won was the one who had the greatest number of oath-helpers. The custom is not unique in Greek history; it finds an analogy in the old Germanic and English custom of compurgation.[65]

With the promulgation of law-codes, the Greek judicial system made one step forward; the oath was still an essential part of the evidence; relatives and friends were oath-helpers (if we may call them such), but their oath now supported the deposition of the principal. Formerly, the oath-helpers had not needed to know the facts; now, they had to have some knowledge of them.

In the judicial procedure of Gortyn there seem to have been three categories of witnesses: (i) the rarest type of witnesses admitted in the court was the oath-helpers, who supported by oath the statement of the party;[66] (ii) a more common category admitted in the court was the instrumental witnesses, who had to support their own statement by an oath;[67] (iii) the most common witnesses were the *martyres,* who apparently declared only the facts as they knew them.[68]

It is evident that the law of Gortyn represents a transitional stage in the use of the oath for witnesses. In regard to the first category, there was an effort to minimize the use of oath-helpers, whose oath was considered to be evidence, i.e., decisory. In the second, the oath had become obligatory-confirmatory. In the third, there is no certainty whether the oath was still obligatory or merely voluntary, though the testimony itself was obligatory.

In Athens, the gradual secularization of the oath can be traced with some certainty. At first, the oath was the evidence; then it had to support the evidence; finally, it was no longer required by law, that is, it became voluntary.

In a fifth century (409-8 B.C.) inscription,[69] which is believed to bear the homicide laws of Draco, it appears that the most distant relatives, cousins, in-laws and members of the phratry concur to the prosecution (*syndiokein*). These are not simply witnesses to confirm, in case of need, the deposition made by the closest rela-

65. J. W. Jones, *op. cit.*, pp. 138-39. Bonner and Smith, *op. cit.*, vol. 2, p. 174 f.

66. *Law of Gortyn,* III, 49-52. Also, II, 35-45.

67. *Law of Gortyn,* IX, 37-40.

68. *Law of Gortyn,* II, 17-20. Also, I, 14-23; IX, 44, 51.

69. Tod, 87. *Syll.*,[3] 111.

tive. The obligation and the right to prosecute extends even to them. There could be no compromise with the murderer and his family if one member alone opposed it: "The interdiction against the murderer shall be made in the agora by the closest relative. The cousins, in-laws and the members of the phratry shall concur to the prosecution," and "to arrange a compromise, if there is a father, a brother or son, there must be the consent of all; the opposition of one alone shall prevail. If there be no such persons, there must be the unanimous consent of the relatives to the degree of cousins, and they shall all take the oath."

Are these relatives the sworn-in witnesses who depose their own statement and corroborate it by a confirmatory oath, or are they oath-helpers? Dareste, Haussoullier, and Reinach[70] seem to consider them oath-helpers. However, it must be concluded that the information is insufficient for a definite answer.

Solon adopted Draco's rules regarding homicide cases, that is, the relatives of the party supported by oath, in the preliminary hearings, the sworn statement of the principal. Other witnesses might also be required by law to testify, but they took the oath on their own depositions both before the magistrate in the preliminary hearings, and before the court when they confirmed their depositions.[71]

In civil cases, the witnesses, however, were not required by law to take the oath on their depositions either before the magistrate in the preliminary hearings or before the popular judges in the courts. The oath was voluntary.[72] The witness might volunteer to take it or he might take it by way of challenge with the consent of both parties.[73] This oath-challenge, if taken, would have only probative force before the dicasts; everywhere else, including before the arbitrators, it might have either decisory or probative power, according to the agreement of the parties.

Against a recalcitrant witness there were three possible actions: (i) *dike lipomartyriou*,[74] when a witness had promised to depose, but later refused to do so; (ii) *dike blabes*,[75] when a witness, by refusing to testify, withheld such important information that the

70. Dareste, Haussoullier, and Reinach, *op. cit.*, no. XXI.
71. Lysias, 4, 4. Also, Antiphon, 5, 12.
72. Dem. 57, 56.
73. Dem. 29, 26 and 54; 45, 58; 49, 20.
74. Dem. 49, 19.
75. Dem. 49, 20.

party suffered damage; (iii) *graphe prokleseos,*[76] when a witness, having testified in the preliminary hearings, refused to appear in court to confirm his own deposition. No depositions, not even those sworn before the magistrate, could be read in court if the witness were not present to confirm them *in persona.* It was a *graphe,* because the witness was summoned during the trial by a herald, and if he failed to appear, he would be accused of contempt of court, which carried a penalty of a thousand drachmae, payable to the state.[77]

However, a witness could avoid the obligation to testify by the *exomosia,* which was an oath declaring that he knew nothing about the matter in dispute. Testify or take the disclaimer oath (*martyrein e exomnysthai*)[78] was the legal dictum. The *exomosia,* evidently, was final. It exonerated the witness from the obligation to testify, and, because of its great power, it was very solemn. According to Aristotle, it was taken at the oath-rock in the agora.

If a witness could not be present in court, then the party could have him depose before sworn witnesses, who, in turn, would testify in court for the absent witness. Such a sworn testimony was called *ekmartyria.*[79]

Athens had come almost to the end of the road that led the system of proofs to simple juridical deposition, practically free from all religious mixture: the *Areopagus* had kept the obligatory oath to the testimony, but the *Heliae* had adopted the principle of the voluntary oath. The testimony itself, however, remained obligatory: testify or take the oath, or one thousand drachmae fine.

Examples of oath-helpers from places other than Gortyn and Athens are rare and doubtful. Aristotle (*Politics* 1269a) has the best information there is: "Indeed the relics of ancient customs which are still in existence here and there, are utterly absurd; there is, for example, a law at Cyme, relating to homicide, that if an accuser can produce a definite number of witnesses from his own kinsmen, the person accused shall be held guilty." In a fifth-century

76. Aeschines, 1, 46; 2, 68.

77. *Ibid.*

78. Dem. 19, 176; 29, 20; 45, 58-61; 49, 20; 59, 28. Isaeus, 9, 18.

79. Dem. 46, 7. Slaves could not appear in court as witnesses. Their testimony was taken outside the court before witnesses and, in order to be valid, had to be given under torture. Similarly, women and minors could not testify in court. Their testimony also had to be taken outside the court before witnesses. However, they could appear before arbitrators. Cf. Dem. 39, 3 and 18; 40, 41; 29, 26.

inscription[80] from Oeanthea the word *epomotai* is argued by some scholars[81] to mean oath-helpers.

It must be concluded that trial by oath-helpers in homicide cases was used by the Greeks, but such trials must have been rare and almost non-existent by the fourth century.

In civil cases, the best information about the oath of the witnesses is given in the well-known inscription[82] of Cnidus:

i. those witnesses who can be present at the trial shall depose their statements personally before the tribunal;

ii. those who cannot be present shall give their testimony in their city through affidavits before their legal patrons (*prostatai*), and in the presence of the opposing party, if the latter wishes to attend. Before the deposition, the witness shall take the oath prescribed by law, that he will speak the truth and that he is not able to get to court.

Therefore, the witness who could not go before the court, had to make, during the investigation (i.e. *anakrisis*), a deposition under oath, and also excuse himself by oath from being present. This is the same procedure as in Athens: testify or take the oath (*martyrein e exomnysthai*).

80. Tod, 34. C. D. Buck, *op. cit.*, no. 56.

81. G. Glotz, "Jusjurandum," *Darem.-Saglio*. Bonner and Smith, *op. cit.*, vol. 2, p. 184 f. On the other hand, Buck, *op. cit.*, translates the word *epomotai* as jurors rather than as oath-helpers.

82. *Syll.*,[3] 953.

FOUR

The Use of the Oath in International Life

THE OATH IN INTERSTATE RELATIONS. There was no codified international law in ancient Greece. "Faith" (*pistis*) was the underlying basis of all international relationships, the determining factor of all acts of public conduct as well as private; it was the fundamental principle of fairness, equity (*epieikeia*). As a rule, "faith" was reinforced by a solemn oath, and the most common oath-phrases of ancient writers dealing with interstate pacts were: "to give or exchange oaths and faith" (*horkous kai pistin didonai* or *poieisthai*); "to conclude or break oath-bound faith" (*horkia pista temnein* or *delesthai*); and "to conclude a treaty by oaths accompanied with libations and sacrifices" (*spondas kai horkia temnein*).[1]

A violation of the oath in treaties was not only grounds for divine retribution, but also for reprisals, self-help, or war. The oath came to constitute the juridical basis of the whole body of customary practices which regulated international conduct.

1. The word *sponde* must have indicated first the ritual and then, also, the oath. On the other hand, *horkia* must have referred first to the oaths and then, also, to the whole treaty-making ceremony, including the provisions sworn.

A mere promise without being supplemented and confirmed by a fitting religious formula, that is, the oath, was not considered to be necessarily binding. Thus, in 431 B.C., when the Thebans made an abortive attempt to seize Plataea, the Plataeans agreed to release the prisoners if the Thebans withdrew from Plataea's territory. The Thebans accepted the offer and withdrew without doing any injury; but the Plataeans, as soon as they had hastily carried in their property from the country, slaughtered the Theban prisoners, declaring that they had not ratified the agreement by an oath.[2] Similarly, Philip's campaign against Thrace could not be impugned on a juridical basis, because the peace negotiations that were being carried out with Athens in 346 B.C. had not yet been sealed by the oaths; for the oaths, as mentioned above, were necessary for the fulfillment of the contract. Philip's move was of doubtful faith, but certainly not a formal breach of the peace treaty.[3]

It was not until later, especially during Hellenistic times, that the oath gradually gave way to the private or public seal (*sphragis*) and signature of the parties or delegates. This was probably due to a decline of concern in public religion and to a rising interest in mystical religions, which on account of their personal and intimate nature were somewhat divorced from the public aspects of life. Furthermore, the tremendous rise of diplomatic, commercial, and social activity demanded a less cumbersome procedure than the ceremonialism of the oath. The new procedure was provided by the availability of more expeditious means of guarantee, such as the widespread use of writing.

One of the earliest oath-formulae in peace treaties which has been preserved is that of the fifty year truce between Athens and Sparta in 421 B.C., known as the Peace of Nicias. The following is Thucydides' report (5, 17): "They [the Lacedaemonians] made the agreement, ratifying it by libations and oaths with the Athenians and the Athenians with them. . . ." After mentioning the conditions of the peace, Thucydides (5, 18) continues: "the oath shall be as follows: 'I will abide by the terms of this treaty, justly and without deceit. . . .' Both parties shall renew the oath year by year."

2. Thucydides, 2, 5: "The Thebans . . . say that the Plataeans took the oath; but the Plataeans . . . deny that they took the oath."

3. Dem. 7, 36.

It can be argued that this formula was not the actual one of the oath, but a Thucydidean précis of it: the conditions are properly stated, but there is no invocation of the gods and no sanction, both of which are essential elements for the ritual of the oath-formula.

The personal pronoun in the oath brings up the question of the degree to which individual magistrates represented the polis, or rather, the citizen body. This question is connected with the issue of the juridical identity of the polis, discussed in Chapter Two. The individual magistrates, without any doubt, acted as representatives of the citizen body. But in regard to the execution of the obligations involved in the treaties, the oath seems to have bound the individual official, sometimes personally and sometimes with a few eminent citizens, but often in company with the whole citizen body. It must have been for this reason that the oath was occasionally administered to as many citizens as possible, and sometimes even the whole citizen body.[4] The purpose was to replace general, collective responsibility by individual responsibility, to emphasize the direct individual involvement in political matters.

Another example of early oath-formulae is that sworn in the treaty of alliance between Athens and subject allies on one side, and the Argives, Mantineans, and Eleans on the other. The alliance was made in 420 B.C. and was inscribed on a slab which, unfortunately, is in a fragmentary state.[5] Thucydides' rendering (5, 47)[6] of this alliance is as follows: "The Athenians shall swear to the treaty for themselves and their allies, but the Argives, Mantineans and Eleans and their allies shall swear to it individually by states. And they shall each swear the oath that is most binding in their own country, over full-grown victims. And the oath shall be as follows: 'I will abide by the alliance in accordance with its stipulations, justly and without injury and without guile, and will not transgress it by any art or device.' "

Two points are of particular interest in this oath. The first arises in the clause: "The Athenians shall swear to the treaty for themselves and their allies, whereas the Argives, Mantineans, Eleans and their allies shall swear to it individually by states." The sig-

4. J. W. Jones, *op. cit.*, pp. 154-56. Vinogradoff, *op. cit.*, 107, 162, and 242.
5. Tod, 72.
6. See Tod's comments (*op cit.*, vol. 1, p. 177) on the slight discrepancies between the inscription and Thucydides' version.

nificance of this is that the allies of Athens were *de facto* subject to Athens in foreign relations. The following historical incident may illustrate the point by way of contrast. When, in the peace conference of 373 B.C., Epaminondas demanded that the Theban delegation should take the oath on behalf of the Theban league, Sparta refused to allow it, because she would not recognize Thebes' sovereignty in Boeotia.

The second point arises in the clause: "They shall each swear the oath that is most binding in their own country." This again brings up the question of the local individualization of the *theoi horkioi*, which has been discussed in Chapter One.

In addition to the treaties among Greek city-states, there were the leagues, such as the amphictyonic, hegemonic, and federal leagues. Here, too, the charters were incorporated in the oath-formula. The word amphictyony was applied to a religious union of a number of states; the center of the amphictyony was the shrine of a god. The best known amphictyony was the Delphic; its members, as might be expected, were bound together by oath. Some fragments of the oath are found in Aeschines (2, 115): "At the same time, I reviewed, from the beginning, the history of the founding of the sacred place and the first congress of the amphictyonic members that was ever held; I read their oaths, in which they swore that they would destroy no amphictyonic city, nor would they shut them off from running water either in war or in peace; that if anyone should violate this oath, they would march against them and raze their city; and if anyone should rob the property of the god, or be accessory to it, or plot against the holy places, they would punish him with hand, foot, voice and all their might. To this oath was added a heavy curse."

The obligation of this oath, therefore, was the basis of any military action by the members of the amphictyony, either against disobedient members or foreign enemies of the sanctuary, and, consequently, the basis of a certain degree of international organization.[7]

In 596 B.C., for example, the oracle, according to Aeschines (3, 107-112), urged the members of the amphictyony to abide by the oath and punish the Cirrhaeans, who "had repeatedly com-

7. A. J. H. Greenidge, *A Handbook of Greek Constitutional History* (Oxford, 1920), p. 48. Cf. I. Calabi, *Ricerche sui Rapporti fra le Poleis* (Firenze, 1953).

mitted sacrilege against the temple of Delphi" by stealing the votive offerings, and by outrages "against the amphictyons themselves by imposing exorbitant tolls upon the pilgrims to Delphi." Cirrhae was then leveled to the ground (585 B.C.) and the territory consecrated to the god with a mighty oath: "If anyone should transgress this oath, whether city, private individual or tribe, let them be accursed by Apollo, Artemis, Leto and Athena Forethought. May their land bear no fruit, their wives bring forth no children like their parents, but monsters, their herds yield no increase after their kind; may they suffer defeat in war, in court and councils; may they perish utterly, themselves, their houses and their whole race; may they never offer pure sacrifice to Apollo, to Artemis, to Leto and to Athena Forethought; may these gods never accept their offerings."

And again, in 357 B.C., when Aeschines (3, 118-121) denounced the Amphissians for cultivating part of the Cirrhaean land which had been consecrated to the god of Delphi, he urged the congress of the amphictyony to abide by the oath of their forefathers. As a result, a disastrous war broke out (357-46 B.C.), which brought about not only the ruin of the Phocian Amphissians, but also the intervention of Philip II of Macedon, who then established a firm grip on Greek politics by replacing the Phocians in the amphictyonic council.

In hegemonic leagues, however, three things stand out clearly. First, there was the duality of their structure—the hegemonic state and the allies. This duality rested juridically upon oaths taken by the leading state with each of the allies. The formula of the oath determined the duty of the hegemon to protect the allies, and of the allies to follow the hegemon in war. To secede was a violation of the oath-formula, i.e., a breach of contract, since the oath was law to the sworn parties.

Second, there was a tendency for the hegemon[8] to usurp the whole supreme power of the league in making decisions about foreign affairs, which was a violation of a basic element of the Greek polis, the *eleutheria*, i.e., independence in foreign affairs. *De iure* the hegemon claimed to be simply *primus inter pares*, because it contributed most to the league. *De facto* the hegemon made the policies of the league and carried them out. There was likewise a tendency for the hegemon to interfere in the internal affairs

8. Thucydides, 1, 97-99; 6, 43; 7, 57.

of the members, which was a violation of the other basic element of the Greek polis, the *autonomia*, i.e., self-imposed laws, freedom in internal affairs. The hegemon not only provided the military leaders, but also the administrators of the league. It was tempting, then, for the administrators to call upon the military leaders in order to enforce contributions on recalcitrant members. This compulsion was felt to be an infringement of the sovereignty of the members. To overcome this resentment, the hegemon set up, in such recalcitrant allies, a *politeia*, which supported its policies.[9]

Third, there was the lack of common citizenship among the league members.

In fifth- and fourth-century Greece, there were several examples of hegemonic leagues, but the one which set the precedent in becoming an empire of the hegemon was the first Athenian league. It was founded in 477-6 B.C., and the oath-formula of the alliance between Athens and the member-states may be considered its sacred charter.

Unfortunately, none of the league-oaths has been preserved; but there is an inscription[10] which records the alliance between Athens and Corcyrae in 375 B.C., that is, at the time when Athens was about to rebuild its second league. This inscription may give an idea of the formulae sworn by the members of the first league. One important characteristic of the oath, for our purposes, is the fact that the Corcyraeans now swear by the Athenian *theoi horkioi*: Zeus-Apollo-Demeter. The following was the oath of the Athenians: "I shall give aid to the people of the Corcyraeans with all my strength to the best of my ability, if anyone for the purpose of war, either by land or by sea, go against the territory of the Corcyraeans, in accordance with whatever notification the Corcyraeans shall send; and as concerning war and peace, I shall act in accordance with whatever may seem good to the full body of the allies, and other things I shall do in accordance with the resolutions of the allies. These things I shall do, so help me Zeus and Apollo and Demeter. To me, if I keep my oath, may there be blessings; if not, the opposite." And this was, in turn, the oath of the Corcyraeans: "I shall give aid to the people of the Athenians

9. Pseudo-Xenophon, *Constitution of Athens.*

10. *Syll.*,[3] 151. Tod, 127. Trans. from *Hellenic Civilization*, eds. G. W. Botsford and E. G. Sihler, 2nd ed. (New York, 1920) (hereafter referred to as *HC*), p. 396, no. 122.

with all my strength to the best of my ability, if anyone for the purpose of war, either by land or by sea, go against the territory of the Athenians, in accordance with whatever notification the Athenians shall send; and as concerning war and peace, I shall act in accordance with whatever may seem good to the full body of the allies, and other things I shall do in accordance with the resolutions of the Athenians and the allies. These things I shall do, so help me Zeus and Apollo and Demeter. To me, if I keep my oath, may there be blessings; if not, the opposite."

Aristotle (*Const. of Athens,* 23), referring to the first Athenian league of 477-6 B.C., adds that Aristides dramatized the perennial nature of the bonds of the oath by throwing iron bars into the sea as part of the ritualistic ceremony of the oath. The oath was a contract between Athens and each of the allies. It formed the juridical basis of the union,[11] and this meant that attempts to secede would be regarded as violations of the oath and as acts against the Hellenic cause. In fact, what else but the oath could have given Athens the legal basis forcibly to prevent Naxos[12] from seceding in 466 B.C.? This was not a war but a police action, and similar police actions, based on the juridical force of the oath, were taken against Erythrae in 455 B.C., against Chalcis in 446 B.C., and against various others who attempted to secede.

According to I. Calabi,[13] in fact, Aristotle's phrase (*Const. of Athens,* 23, 5) "to have the same enemy and friend" in reference to the Delian league meant to bind one another in such an agreement that no member might any longer declare war independently, a thing which, for instance, the members of the Peloponnesian league could still do. Therefore, the Delian alliance was not only for retaliation against Persia and to free those Greek cities which were still under the Persians, but also against any future enemy who might even be and, in fact, eventually was, Greek. This fact diminishes greatly the possibility of seeing in the founding charter of the Delian league a manifestation of panhellenic solidarity. Thus, the league was established with the immediate purpose of freeing the Greek cities, but Athens later used it to increase her

11. A. J. H. Greenidge, *op. cit.*, p. 193 f.

12. Thucydides, 1, 98: "After these things they waged war against the Naxians who had seceded from the league and reduced them by siege. This was the first allied city to be enslaved in contravention of the agreement, then followed the enslavement of the rest as each case occurred."

13. I. Calabi, *op. cit.*, p. 45 f.

power. The clause, then—to have the same friend and the same enemy—really came to mean that the allies should have the same enemies and the same friends as the mistress city. The hegemon city turned to her advantage the anti-Persian propaganda, just as a century and a half later, Philip II of Macedon would do when he founded the league of Corinth.

The institution of the tribute (*phoros*) over the members of the Delian league by Athens had no precedent among the Greek leagues; it was an oriental innovation. Croesus had imposed it on the Greek cities of Asia Minor and the Persians inherited it. In principle, the tribute paid by the members constituted a contract under which Athens undertook to ensure their defense. But, in reality, tribute (*phoros*) and freedom (*eleutheria*) were contrasting ideas: the *phorou hypoteleis* (tributaries) were *hypekooi* (subjects). To say, however, that Athens deliberately planned to replace Persia would be hard to believe, but it is possible that the example of tribute paid to the Persians influenced the organization of the new league.

There can be little doubt that by the outbreak of the Peloponnesian war the process of transforming the Delian league into an Athenian empire was complete, and that this transformation was the deliberate aim of the Athenian democrats, especially Pericles. In fact, the synod no longer met; the treasury of the league had been moved from Delos to Athens; the jurisdiction of the Athenian courts in important criminal cases and commercial suits had been extended over all the members of the league; pro-Athenian democratic regimes were established practically in all subject cities; and, finally, the cleruchies, that is, nuclei of Athenian citizens, settled under generous terms on confiscated property, formed for all practical purposes a sort of Athenian garrison in several of the subject communities.

The Athenian decree[14] (probable date 453-2 B.C.) concerning the constitution of Erythrae, found on a block of marble on the Acropolis, demonstrates the Athenian attitude, which regarded the cities of the league more as municipalities of the Athenian government than as sovereign allies. It runs as follows:

"The Erythraeans shall bring to the greater Panathenaea offerings worth not less than three minas. . . .

"There shall be a council of the Erythraeans, filled by lot and

14. *Syll.*,[3] 41. Tod, 29. Trans. from *HC*, p. 260, no. 71.

consisting of one hundred and twenty men. A man so appointed shall undergo scrutiny before the council, and it shall not be lawful for anyone under thirty years of age to be a councillor. Those who are disqualified shall be liable to prosecution and shall not be councillors within four years. The council shall be drawn by lot and established at present by the Athenian overseers (*episcopoi*) and commander of the garrison, in the future by the council in office and the Athenian commandant.

"Each one of those who are to be councillors at Erythrae shall, before entering office, swear by Zeus, Apollo and Demeter, imprecating destruction upon himself and upon his children if he commits perjury; and he shall swear the oath upon burning sacrifices. The councillors shall compel the performance of these things; and if they fail to do so, they may be fined one thousand drachmae or whatever sum the Erythraean people may decree for them to pay. The councillors shall swear in the following terms:

" 'I will be councillor as well and truly as I am able for the people of the Erythraeans, Athenians and of the allies.

" 'And I will not revolt against the commonwealth of the Athenians, nor against the allies of the Athenians, either of my own accord or at the will of another.

" 'Neither will I desert them, either of my own accord or at the will of another.

" 'Neither will I receive back, either of my own accord or at the will of another, anyone of those who fled to the Medes, except with the sanction of the Athenians and of the Erythraean people.

" 'Neither will I drive away any who are remaining, except with the sanction of the Athenians and of the People.'

"If any Erythraean shall kill another Erythraean, let him be put to death. If anyone shall be condemned to perpetual banishment, let him be banished from the Athenian alliance, and let his property be confiscated by the Erythraeans.

"If anyone is convicted of attempting to betray the city of the Erythraeans to the tyrants, let him be put to death, both himself and his children, unless his children are shown to be favorably disposed towards the Erythraean people and the Athenians. The children, after surrendering the property of the convicted, shall receive one half of it back, and the other half shall be confiscated.

"The same shall be the case if anyone is convicted of attempting to betray the Athenian people or the garrison at Erythrae."

In this inscription, three main points seem to stand out distinctly: the establishment of a democratic *politeia* by the Athenian commissioners, which was an infringement of sovereignty in the internal affairs of the allies; the administration to the Erythraeans of a new oath of allegiance to Athens and the subject allies of Athens, i.e., to the Athenian empire; and the use of the Athenian triad of the oath-gods (Zeus-Apollo-Demeter) in the oath of the Erythraeans.

The nature of this last obtrusion was full of important implications, for if the league was simply a union of sovereign states, then it would not need special protecting gods, because the union meant also alliance of the gods of each sovereign state,[15] and each party would have sworn either its own local, legal oath in accordance with the ancestral customs, or a new formula which combined the oath-gods of the two parties. But if Athens was aiming to transform a loose alliance into a political community, or better into an empire, then this new community would need special protecting deities and an eponymous god. It is a fact that the Athenians were trying to make Athens not only a cultural center, but also a politico-religious center.[16] Plutarch (*Pericles* 17) says that Pericles urged the Athenians to have lofty thoughts (*mega phronein*) and to think of themselves as worthy of great endeavors. So, in 448-47 B.C., he launched his famous proposal to all Greek nations for a congress to be held at Athens in order to deliberate on the freedom of the sea (by now an Athenian domain!) and on the rebuilding of the sanctuaries (namely, the Athenian temples, such as that of Eleusis of the Goddesses Twain and those on the Acropolis) destroyed by the Persians.[17] The panhellenic summit meeting, as expected, was torpedoed by Sparta and the Peloponnesian league. Nevertheless, the failure of the meeting did not dissuade Athens from pursuing her bid for national ascendancy. She proceeded to build the temples with her money (or with that of the league?), to erect on the Acropolis the "Altar of Greece" (to paraphrase Aeschylus' lines in the *Eumenides*, 920-25), and to make herself the "School of Hellas" (to quote Pericles' speech in Thucydides). In 423 B.C. Clearchus' decree on the internationalization of

15. Ziebarth, "Eid," *RE*.

16. M. P. Nilsson, *op. cit.*, vol. 1, pp. 691-701.

17. Plutarch, *Pericles*, 17. For the credibility of Plutarch's information see I. Calabi, *op. cit.*, p. 69 f.

the Athenian coinage, weights, and measures throughout the empire clearly revealed the nature of Pericles' "lofty thoughts," *viz.*, to establish Athenian leadership also in the financial and commercial spheres of the Greek world. In 418 B.C. Athens again made her bid as a religious center: she issued a proclamation[18] that regulated the offerings of the first fruits to the Goddesses Twain of Eleusis on the part of the Athenians, compelled the allies to conform to the same regulations, and then went on to invite all other Hellenes to make similar offerings, despite the fiasco of the congress of 448-47 B.C. Finally, the capture of Melos, the great expedition against Sicily, and the memorable speech of Alcibiades at Sparta about Athen's ambitions leave hardly any doubt that Athens was vigorously pursuing Pericles' imperialistic "lofty thoughts" (*mega phronein*). The dramatists, on their part, also, set about building the myth that claimed the kinship of all the Ionians, who formed a large family with Ion as common ancestor or eponymous god, and Athens as mother country.

Another Athenian decree (446 B.C.), similar to that dealing with Erythrae, concerns the new relationship between Athens and Chalcis,[19] which had also tried to secede from the league. The following quotation includes only the oaths of each party:

"Be it resolved by the council and by the people. Antiochus was the prytanizing tribe. Dracontides was chairman. Diognetus moved the resolution: that the council and the jurors of the Athenians shall swear the oath in the following terms:

" 'I will not expel the Chalcideans from Chalcis or destroy their city;

" 'And I will not punish any private citizen with loss of civil rights or with exile, or give judgment of arrest or of death or of confiscation of goods against him without trial, except by (authority of) the Athenian people;

" 'And I will not put to vote (a motion) against either the com-

18. *Syll.*,[3] 83. Tod, 74. Trans. in *HC,* p. 354, no. 106. The religious offerings of the allied cities were not required as part of the tribute, but as a symbol of their relation to Athens, which in this respect, as Tod remarks, was similar to that of the *cleruchies* (colonies of Athenian citizens). So the allies took part in the sacrificial festivities and had to present the Eleusinian goddesses the same tribute of grain as did the Athenians: on every hundred *medimnoi* of barley a *hekteus,* and on every hundred *medimnoi* of wheat a *hemiekteon.*

19. *Syll.*,[3] 64. Tod, 42. Trans. from *HC,* p. 262, no. 72.

munity or any private citizen (of Chalcis), when a summons has not been issued against them;

" 'And if an embassy comes, I will introduce it to the council and the people within ten days, when I am a prytanis, to the best of my ability;

" 'And I will maintain these things for the Chalcideans, if they are obedient to the Athenian people.'

"An embassy from Chalcis shall administer the oath to the Athenians with the help of the Commissioners of Oaths, and shall register (the names of) those who swear it. Let the generals see to it that all swear.

"The Chalcideans shall swear in the following terms:

" 'I will not revolt against the Athenian people by any art or device, either in word or in deed; and I will not follow one who undertakes to revolt, and if anyone incites to revolt, I will denounce him to the Athenians;

" 'I will pay the tribute to the Athenians, as I may induce them (to assess it);

" 'And I will be to them as good and true an ally as I can;

" 'I will aid and succor the Athenian people, if anyone wrongs the Athenian people;

" 'And I will be obedient to the Athenian people.'

"All the men of Chalcis who are of age shall swear; and if anyone shall not swear, he shall lose his civil rights (*atimia*); his property shall be confiscated, and a tenth of it shall be consecrated to Olympian Zeus. An Athenian embassy shall go to Chalcis and administer the oath with the help of the Commissioners of Oaths in Chalcis, and shall register (the names of) the Chalcideans who swear."

The decree ends with the following paragraph: "The Chalcideans may inflict punishments upon their own citizens at Chalcis just as the Athenians (do on theirs) at Athens, excepting exile, death, or loss of civil rights, concerning which there shall be an appeal to Athens to the courts of the thesmothetae according to the decree of the people."

It is evident that the oaths of this decree are contracts, not between equals, but between hegemon and subject: the oath of the Chalcideans is essentially an oath of allegiance to the Athenian demos. In criminal cases, the Chalcideans had to appeal to Athenian courts. Evidently this clause reduces Chalcis to the status of subject municipality, with restricted freedom also in internal affairs; a municipality, because Chalcis had lost its sovereignty totally in foreign matters (*eleutheria*) and partially in internal matters (*autonomia*); a subject, because it did not enjoy full Athenian citizenship.

Another important characteristic of this decree was the fact that the Chalcideans now swore "obedience to the Athenian people," whereas in the decree of Erythrae we noticed that the Erythraeans still swore allegiance to the "Athenians and the allies."

There can be no question about the fact that, by the last quarter of the fifth century, the members of the league were, *de facto,* more or less "sworn-in" to a pro-Athenian (namely, democratic) *politeia* and to obedience to the Athenian *demos.* Perhaps Athens had no desire to intervene in the internal political struggle of members of the league, to encroach upon their autonomy. But when these members exploded into civil war and the partisans of the oligarchic party began to negotiate with Sparta, the leader of the oligarchic block in the Greek world, then Athens, as leader not only of the Delian league but also of the democratic block, had really no other choice but to respond to the appeal of the democrats and assure their control of the government.

Philip of Macedon, similarly, after the battle of Chaeronea in 338 B.C., used the victory for two purposes: to give the Greeks internal peace (*koine eirene*) by establishing an international council (*koinon synedrion*), and to unite them in a crusade (*symmachia*) of revenge against Persia.

The oath-formula, which constituted the charter of the league, was found in an inscription[20] on the Acropolis; it runs as follows:

"I swear by Zeus, Ge, Helios, Poseidon, Athena, Ares and all the gods and goddesses.

"I will remain in peace and will not break the agreement with Philip of Macedon.

"I will not bear arms for the purpose of injury against any of those that abide by the oaths, either by land or by sea.

"I will not seize for the purpose of war a city or a fort or harbor belonging to any of those that share in the peace, by any art or device whatsoever.

"I will not overthrow the kingship of Philip and his descend-

20. *Syll.*,[3] 260. Tod, 177. Trans. from *HC*, p. 420, no. 128.

ants or the governments existing in the respective states at the time when they swore the oaths regarding the peace.

"I will do nothing contrary to this treaty either in person or by allowing another, in so far as I can prevent it.

"And if anyone shall commit any violation of the agreement, I will give aid to those who need it at the time, according as they may demand.

"And I will make war upon him who violates the general peace, according as it may be required of me and the commander-in-chief may order. . . ."

Thus, Philip's oath also emphasized the reciprocal agreements of nonaggression among the members of the league and the sanctions against violators. It further ensured the maintenance of general peace and the pledge of the single city-states to subvert neither the constitution of others nor their own.

The novelty of this oath, however, consisted in the fact that it was taken also by Philip in his capacity as a representative of both the people of Macedonia and the dynasty; that Philip's pledge to respect the existing constitutions of the contracting states had as a counterpart the allies' pledge of fealty to Philip and his decendants; and, finally, that the title of hegemon given to Philip sealed the hegemony of Macedon over Greece.

This oath was thus a new political formula in Greece. Not surprisingly, it was expressed in traditional words and forms, but the old balance of power among the city-states was gone forever, for Philip's oath became a precedent not only for the oath of allegiance to the Hellenistic kings, but also for that to the Roman emperor.

The federal leagues were distinguished from the amphictyony by the presence of central authorities of a political and military character, and from the symmachy by their actual unity. The federal leagues included a dual citizenship, local and federal. They appeared from the end of the fourth century B.C., and had a religious center, as might be expected, since they formed a community and not a simple alliance. The oath-formula was the constitutional charter as well as a pledge of allegiance.

In conclusion, the sanctions for the obligations in treaties were fines, hostages and, especially, solemn oaths. Oaths, in fact, were the main guarantee of the fulfillment of the conditions of treaties. Fear of the oath's religious sanction and imprecation was certainly a strong deterrent, but like all deterrents, it did not prevent breaches of faith under temptation. So the parties began more and more to feel the need of military and police actions to supplement divine justice; and, consequently, the oaths, ceasing to be merely rigid ritualistic formulae, grew into veritable legal charters.

THE OATH IN INTERNATIONAL ARBITRATION. The Greeks, despite their primitive political exclusiveness and struggle for hegemony, very early adopted a machinery of diplomacy, *viz.*, international congresses, foreign lobbyists (*proxenoi*), and treaties providing for commercial redresses (*dosidikia* or *dikaiodosia, dikai apo symbolon*) in which both principles of *forum contractus* and *forum rei* were recognized; and provisions to refer future disputes to an international arbitration were often inserted in the treaties of peace and alliance.[21]

The following is an early example of an agreement among the Ionians to arbitrate their differences in the future: "During the course of this year (i.e., the end of the Ionian revolt)," says Herodotus (6, 42), "no further hostile measures were undertaken by the Persians against Ionia; on the contrary, they took measures which were greatly to its advantage: Artaphernes, governor of Sardis, sent for representatives from all Ionian States and forced them to bind themselves by oath to settle their differences by arbitration, instead of being continually at daggers drawn."

The ordinary procedure was first to select an umpire, either a foreign statesman like Themistocles, or, more often, a city (*ekkletos polis*) in whose impartiality both parties had confidence.[22] However, in cases involving the members of a league, the hegemon city obtained or usurped the right of judgment. Then, the litigant parties took an oath to abide by the award. Sometimes a further guarantee was given to the oath, namely, securities or fines. But there was no international army or police force. This, doubtless, explains the limited success of international arbitration.[23] Certain

21. Thucydides, 1, 78, 85, 140, 144; 4, 118; 5, 18, 79; 7, 18.

22. Herodotus, 5, 95. Thucydides, 1, 28; 5, 41. Tod, 33.

23. However, M. N. Tod, *International Arbitration amongst the Greeks* (Oxford, 1913), pp. 186-88, commenting on the success of arbitration in ancient Greece, concludes that in the great majority of cases arbitration brought an immediate and lasting cure; in a small minority there was temporary alleviation only: out of 81 cases of arbitration 33 were permanently settled by a single court decision, eight required further arbitration.

Spartan leaders,[24] for instance, thought it shameful to submit to unbiased but militarily insignificant Hellenic states, such as Megara, and, consequently, were believed to prefer force to arbitration if their interests were at stake.

From the defeat of Chaeronea down to the time of Roman rule, international arbitration became very frequent, and the epigraphical evidence is abundant.[25] Philip, Alexander the Great, the Diadochoi, and the Roman Senate made it clear that their direct or indirect arbitration was binding. The sanction of the oath was left not only to the wrath of the gods, but also to these earthly powers.

The arbitration was conducted in a sanctuary, and the members of the court took an oath over sacrificial victims, as was the universal practice in Greek courts of law. The classic example of international arbitration is that of Cnidus (second century B.C.), which had been invited by Calymna and Cos to settle a dispute between them. The formula of the oath taken by the members of the Cnidean Tribunal has been cited in Chapter Three.

The following is the oath of the Delphian amphictyonies who had been called to arbitrate on a land dispute between Amphissa and Anticyra-Ambryssus-Delphi:

"Every question in the judgment relating to the treasury and the boundaries of Apollo, I will decide as is true to the best of my belief.

"I will not give false judgment for the sake of favor or enmity.

"And the sentence, passed in accordance with the judgment, I will enforce to the best of my power with all possible speed.

"And I will make just restoration to the god.

"Nor will I receive gifts, neither myself nor anyone else on my behalf.

"Nor will I give any of the common money to anyone nor receive it myself.

"These things will I do.

"If I swear truly, may I have blessings, but if I swear falsely,

24. Plutarch, *Apophthegmata* 215C: "Agesipolis, the son of Pausanias, when the Athenians proposed the arbitration of Megara concerning some complaints about each other, said: 'it is a shame, men of Athens, that those who led the Greeks should know less about justice than the Megarians.' "

25. M. N. Tod, *International Arbitration amongst the Greeks, passim.* C. Phillipson, *The International Law and Custom of Ancient Greece and Rome*, 2 vols. (London, 1911), *passim.*

may Themis, Pythian Apollo, Leto, Artemis, Histia, Eternal Fire and all the gods and goddesses take from me salvation by a dreadful doom; may they permit myself and all my race to enjoy neither children, nor crops, nor fruits, nor property; and may they cast me forth in my lifetime from the possessions which I now have."[26]

In conclusion, the oath was a *condicio sine qua non* of any judicial proceedings. As in civil courts, judge, witness and litigant each had to take his respective oath; the judges to be impartial, the witnesses to corroborate their testimony, the litigants to defend their cause conscientiously.

26. M. N. Tod, *International Arbitration amongst the Greeks*, p. 116.

FIVE

The Use of the Oath in Social Life

IT HAS ALREADY BEEN MENTIONED that the Greek people lived completely in a politico-religious environment. Not only their public but also their private life was spent in the immediate presence of the gods, so all their actions fell one way or the other under the jurisdiction of some god and, consequently, they were also to some extent religious acts. The oath, therefore, was not restricted to their political activity, but extended also to their social life. Here, too, since the oath was very common, it is necessary to limit the discussion to certain major aspects of social life.

THE PHRATRY. The phratry, as we have mentioned in Chapter Two, was a socio-religious organization. Membership in it, however, determined the legitimacy of a child and, thus, was probably a prerequisite not only to citizenship but also to candidacy for office.[1]

1. Aristotle, *Const. of Athens*, 55, 2-3. Cf. C. Hignett, *op. cit.*, p. 56: "The list kept by each deme only included male citizens who had attained their eighteenth year. Thus, the phratry-lists, which may be regarded as ecclesiastical registers independent of the civil registers kept on behalf of the state by demes, provided the only record of the citizen-rights of women and minors; moreover, an adult male, if his right to appear on the list of his deme was questioned, could plead his membership of a phratry as proof of his status."

In fact, the individual had not been completely emancipated from his phratry. The concentric circles (family, phratry, tribe) in which the individual originally was enclosed had not been entirely broken up by the state. The secular struggle between the centripetal forces of the state and the centrifugal forces of the religious and family units did not quite end in the absolute supremacy of the state, but rather in the incorporation of these religious and family units into the organization of the state. So, the phratry maintained a socio-religious life of its own. It formed a corporate group with legislative, judicial, and executive powers; it had its own Zeus or Apollo Patroos or Phratrios, and its own shrines. Briefly, it represented in miniature the political organization of the polis, and the individual still grew up, to some extent, within the socio-religious atmosphere of the phratry system.

An inscription[2] from Delphi, dated around 400 B.C., deals with the phratry of the Labyadai and, fortunately, bears the oath of its officials. The oath of the officers (*tagoi*) runs as follows:

"I will fulfill the functions of the tagos with justice, in conformity with the laws of the city and of the Labyadai. . . .

"I will enter the revenues and will render an account to the Labyadai with justice, and I will not embezzle nor damage by any subterfuge whatsoever anything that belongs to the Labyadai.

"I will administer the oath to the tagoi of the coming year according to the law.

"I pledge myself by Zeus Patroos; faithful to my oath, many blessings to me; perjurer, many misfortunes."

The inscription also emphasizes the point that "no one, if he had not taken the oath, could be a tagos."

The charter, furthermore, prescribes that the members themselves of the phratry "having sworn by Apollo, Poseidon Phratrios and Zeus Patroos, shall vote with justice and according to the laws of the Delphians. They shall also pray the gods to grant good fortune to those who vote with justice, misfortune to those who vote against justice."

An almost contemporary inscription,[3] dealing with the Athenian phratry of the Demotionidai, gives the oath of those chosen for judicial functions:

2. Dareste, Haussoullier, and Reinach, *op. cit.*, no. XXVIII. Schwyzer, *op. cit.*, no. 323.

3. *Syll.*,[3] 921. Trans. from *HC*, no. 144, p. 471.

"If any of those (candidates for the membership of the phratry) who may be rejected shall desire to appeal to the Demotionidai, they shall have the right; and the house of the Decelians shall choose five men over thirty years of age as council to oppose the appeal. These men shall swear before the phratriarch and the priest that they will advocate what is wholly upright, and that they will not allow anyone without the proper qualifications to be a member of the phratry."

Associations, Clubs, and Guilds. For the Greeks, a corporate association had to have some quality of sanctity. The formation of a purely commercial group of the modern kind would have seemed unhallowed and to have had some indefinable smack of impiety about it.[4] Loyalty to the group idea as an abstraction needed something concrete embodying it, some person, and this person was a deity or a departed founder deified for this purpose. According to Vinogradoff, "the super-individual element of corporative existence is provided not by abstraction from the rights and liabilities of its members, but by personification in the concrete form of Hero-worship."[5] "In this," Vinogradoff continues, "they [the associations] were similar to the City which they imitated in their organization."[6]

The oath of membership was sworn in the god's name. It formed a common bond among the members, since an oath also brought the associating parties together in a common obligation.[7] The officers, besides their oath of membership, also took the oath of investiture upon entering into their terms.

The existence of sworn political clubs (*hetaireiai* and *synomosiai*) is known especially by reason of their abuses. Originally, the *hetaireiai* were associations of friends.[8] But soon the pure solidarity of friends was extended to that of people having common interests. Thus, they came to indicate cultural associations, professional guilds, the intimate circle of a tyrant, the school of a philosopher, the guard and council of the Macedonian kings, even

4. J. W. Jones, *op. cit.*, p. 162.
5. Vinogradoff, *op. cit.*, p. 123.
6. Vinogradoff, *op. cit.*, p. 124.
7. J. W. Jones, *op. cit.*, p. 162.
8. Cf. G. M. Calhoun, *Athenian Clubs in Politics and Legislation* (Austin, 1913). F. Sartori, *Le Eterie nella Vita Politica Ateniese del vi e v secolo A.C.* (Roma, 1959).

military detachments composed of soldiers bound together by special ties.

With the growth of political life there appeared also political *hetaireiai* organized predominantly, but not exclusively, by the upper classes to further their power in the state. Obviously, the nature of such *hetaireiai* varied according to the political principles of the members. They ranged from the extreme right (the oligarchic *hetaireiai*) to the extreme left (the ultra-democratic ones). Some were loosely and quite openly organized, whereas others were tightly and secretly united together.

The *synomosiai*, literally, referred to sworn associations. But the members of the *hetaireiai* also were generally bound by oath. The distinction between the *synomosiai* and the *hetaireiai* must be sought not in the associations per se, nor in their political nature, but in the methods of reaching their goals. The *hetaireiai* were publicly recognized and tolerated, because they operated openly and within the accepted forms of opposition. The *synomosiai*, on the other hand, were outlawed by the state, because their *raison d'être* was the overthrow of the constitution in power by any means; in short, they formed conspiracies against the legitimate authority. All political *hetaireiai* were potentially *synomosiai*. In fact, they became actually such as soon as they went underground in order to overthrow the existing regime. According to Thucydides (8, 54), the oligarchs used them (*hetaireiai* and *synomosiai*) not only to control the courts and the officials, but also to overthrow the democracy: "Peisander, having contacted all the clubs which had happened to exist in the city for the control of the courts and offices, exhorted them to unite and plot the overthrow of the Demos." There can hardly be any doubt that the decree of Demophantus in 410 B.C. (Andocides 1, 96) was aimed precisely against the *hetaireiai* and *synomosiai* of the oligarchs, who evidently were determined to overthrow the democracy by hook or by crook.

Sometimes these clubs, when undertaking an unusually dangerous task, felt that the oath was not sufficient to guarantee the loyalty of the members. On such occasions they supplemented the oath by more grievous bonds, such as complicity in a sacrilege or even assassination, in order that the members, thus incriminated, might be irrevocably bound to the conspiracy. Thus, the profanation of the Eleusinian Mysteries and of the Hermai,[9] the assassination of Hyperbolus,[10] Cleophon,[11] Androcles,[12] Phrynichus[13] and others, were outrages intended to constitute such irrevocable pledges (*pistis*) of fidelity among the members of the conspiracies that they would betray not only their country,[14] but also their relatives. "Moreover," says Thucydides (3, 82), "the ties of blood became weaker than the ties of party, because the party-follower was more ready to dare without pretexts; for such associations are not formed for the advantage of the established laws, but for (personal) aggrandisement in contravention of the established order. They strengthened their pledges to one another not by divine law but by transgressing the law in common. . . ."

Membership in professional guilds was also subordinated to an oath of allegiance. The most famous oath-formula among professional guilds is that of Hippocrates (469-399 B.C.):

"I swear by Apollo the physician, Asclepius, Hygieia, and Panacea and all the gods and goddesses, taking them as witnesses, that I shall fulfill, to the best of my power and ability, the oath and the following obligations:

"I shall consider my teacher of medicine in the same rank as my father.

"I shall share with him my belongings, and if the case arise, I shall provide for his needs.

"I shall consider his children as my brothers, and, if they wish to learn medicine, I shall teach it to them without fee or obligation.

"I shall share the precepts, oral lessons, and the rest of the teachings with my sons, with those of my master, and with the disciples bound by contract and by oath to the medical law, but with none other.

"I shall prescribe the regime of sick people to their advantage,

9. Andocides, 1, 10 and 62.

10. Thucydides, 8, 73.

11. Lysias, 13, 7-12; 30, 10-12.

12. Thucydides, 8, 65: "Some of the younger men, forming a plot, killed secretly a certain Androcles, the most prominent leader of the demos, the man who most of all caused the banishment of Alcibiades." Cf. also, Thucydides, 6, 28 and 89. Andocides, 1, 27. Plutarch, *Alcibiades*, 19.

13. Thucydides, 8, 92.

14. Thucydides, 1, 107: "It seemed best to them (Spartans) to wait in Boeotia and consider how they might safely cross to Peloponnesus. Some Athenians secretly convinced them to this course, hoping to depose the demos and to put a stop to the construction of the long walls."

according to my ability and judgment, and I shall abstain from all evil and injustice.

"I shall not give poison to anyone, if he demands it, nor shall I advise anyone to take it.

"Similarly, I shall not give to any woman a pessary to cause a miscarriage.

"I shall live and exercise my profession in innocence and purity.

"I shall not perform any surgical operation on those suffering from the stone, I shall leave that to those who practise it.

"In any house I enter, I shall enter for the benefit of the sick, avoiding every voluntary corrupting action, especially the seduction of women and young men, free or slaves.

"Whatever I see or hear in society during the practice, or outside the practice of my profession, I shall keep silent on the things which should not be divulged, considering discretion as a duty in such a case.

"If I fulfill this oath without violating it, may it be granted that I enjoy a happy life and profession, honored always among men.

"If I violate it and perjure myself, may the opposite befall me."[15]

CONTRACTS. Oaths most probably sanctioned all legal transactions, and according to the value of the transaction, the oath was either simple or solemn. As a rule, any legal transaction of some importance was performed in public and dominated by more or less rigid formalism. The formalism may be explained to some extent by the wish to ensure the observation of the agreement by a religious sanction, i.e., the curse.

Private contracts. "A contract of buying and selling," says Theophrastus,[16] "is valid in regard to the acquirer when the price is paid and the legal formalities such as the oath, are fulfilled." For instance, again according to Theophrastus,[17] at Aenus, in order to prevent deceit and to make public the change of ownership, the law compelled the buyer of real estate to offer a sacrifice, the importance of which had to be proportionate to the value of

15. Cf. trans. in *HC*, no. 80, p. 298.
16. Stobaeus, *Florilegium*, 44, 22.
17. *Ibid.*

the real estate. Before the altar, in the presence of the magistrate in charge to record the transaction, and of three witnesses from the neighborhood, the buyer swore: "I buy honestly, without collusion, artifice or fraud whatsoever," and the seller swore: "I sell without deceit." Without this formality, apparently, the magistrate could not record the transaction.[18]

According to Plato (Laws 917), at Athens the merchants guaranteed the value of their goods by oath: "Everyone who is guilty of adulteration in the agora, tells a falsehood and deceives, and when he invokes the gods, according to the customs and cautions of the wardens of the agora, he swears without any respect for god or man." According to Isaeus (5, 7), private agreements about inheritance were also ratified by oath: "When they had thus divided up the inheritance, having sworn not to transgress the terms agreed upon, each remained in possession of the share which he had received for twelve years."

Leases, loans, in fact all business transactions were sealed by more or less solemn oaths. Manumission, also, as a sale-contract, was confirmed by oath. Evidently, in manumissions the sale was fictitious, because the sold slave was declared free; but the price, often provided by the slave himself, was real. The sale to the divinity was a detour to give legal form to the sale-contract between master and slave. The slave was not a juridical person, but the god was, and thus was able to buy the slave (often with the slave's money).[19]

Public contracts. Public contracts, like most public transactions, were ratified by oaths. In the already mentioned inscription of Eretria,[20] the contract for the drainage of the swamp was followed by a decree fixing in detail the formalities and the formula of the oath to be taken by the citizens and the epheboi. On his side, the contractor, Chairephanes, was to provide sureties who would guarantee by oaths the execution of the draining and the payment of thirty talents a year after the land had been reclaimed.

A fragmentary papyrus[21] from Hellenistic Egypt has preserved for us the contract between the Queen's officials and the royal cultivators. The contract, as expected, lasts a year during which the cul-

18. Cf. Tod, 25. Aristotle, *Politics* 1321 b.
19. J. W. Jones, *op. cit.*, pp. 283-86 and 307-8.
20. Dareste, Haussoullier, and Reinach, *op. cit.*, no. IX.
21. Trans. from *HC*, no. 186, p. 595 f.

tivator is bound with an oath to the leased land: "In the six-choenix measure of the village, and on this basis also I shall give the produce with honest measure and, up to the time at which I shall measure it out, I shall be present for you and the agents of the queen each day, remaining in the places connected with the work of cultivating the soil . . . without taking advantage of temple, altar, sacred precinct or any sanctuary, nor will I devise any scheme to this sort (to escape my obligations as cultivator). If I keep my oath, may it be well with me, if I break my oath, the opposite."

SIX

Perjury

CONCEPT OF PERJURY. The nature of perjury has been variously explained. Must perjury be applied only to the intention of the oath-taker or to the sworn statement or to both? If an oath-taker swears to do a certain service, but has no intention of keeping his promise, does he commit perjury then and there, or when the time comes to carry out his promise and he does not fulfill his obligation? If an oath-taker swears to do a certain service, but is prevented from keeping his sworn promise by external circumstances, entirely independent of his will, does he commit perjury? Lastly, if an oath-taker swears to the truth of a statement, not knowing it to be false, does he commit perjury?

The most common Greek word for perjury is *epiorkia*, perhaps because the oath-taker stands under the curse of the oath (*epi horkoi*).

According to Homer (*Iliad* 10, 332), Hector swore a false oath (*epiorkon epomose*), even though Dolon's death, which prevented Hector from fulfilling the oath, was entirely independent of Hector's will. In another passage of the *Iliad* (3, 279), the expression *epiorkon omossei*, together with the events, again indicates a false oath. In these instances, it is evident that Homer is not taking into consideration the intention of the oath-takers. The implication is that a perjurer is he who swears an objectively false proposition.

Hesiod (*Theogony* 231), a generation later, apparently takes into consideration the intention of the oath-taker: "god Oath . . . most grieves men on earth when they *wilfully* swear false oaths." And about two and a half centuries later, Herodotus (6, 86) added that even the will to commit perjury, without the deed, would bring down punishment.

However, it was Aristotle who, analysing the *Iliad* 3, 276, first differentiated between perjury of a promissory oath, that is, breaking an oath (*to blaptein ton horkon*) and perjury of an assertory oath, that is, intentionally swearing a false oath (*epiorkia*), and limited *epiorkia* only to the assertory oath. Thus, the Trojans in the above mentioned passage of the *Iliad* must be considered not as perjurers (*epiorkoi*), but merely as oath-breakers, for they failed to keep what they had sworn in good faith.[1]

Cleanthus in the third century B.C. tried to maintain the definition of *epiorkia* for the promissory oath, because the oath-taker, namely, the perjurer, had no intention, at the time when he took the oath, of keeping it: "Cleanthus said that the oath-taker swears rightly (*euorkei*) or swears falsely (*epiorkei*) at the time when he swears: for, if he so swears that he will perform the things in the oath, then he swears rightly (*euorkei*), but if he has the intention of not performing them, then he swears falsely (*epiorkei*)."[2] According to Cleanthus, therefore, in the promissory oath the oath-taker wishes (or does not wish) not only to perform an action in the future, but also to continue to will (or not to will) to perform it until its execution. There is here a twofold will: one is the will actually existing at the moment when the oath is taken; the other is the will to persevere in willing the action until its performance.

Chrysippus (also in the third century B.C.), distinguishing between the assertory oath and promissory oath, affirms that the assertory oath is objectively true or false (*alethorkein* or *pseudorkein*, a terminology which he first introduced), whereas the promissory oath, which deals with the fulfillment of an obligation, is subjectively either good or bad (*euorkon* or *epiorkon*):

1. Cf. K. Latte, "Meineid," *RE*. R. Hirzel, *Der Eid* (Leipzig, 1902), p. 77.
2. Stobaeus, *Florilegium*, 28, 14.

"Chrysippus distinguishes *alethorkein* from *euorkein,* and *pseudorkein* from *epiorkein.* The oath-taker, at the moment when he swears, either *alethorkei* or *pseudorkei,* for the sworn statement (itself) is (objectively) either true or false, because it is an axiom; but the oath-taker swears rightly or falsely not at the time he swears, unless that is also the time to fulfill the obligations of the oath. For one is said to be faithful or unfaithful to an agreement, not when he makes the agreement, but when the time comes to keep the agreement; so, also, one is said to swear rightly (*euorkein*) or falsely (*epiorkein*), when the moment comes to fulfill the things which were agreed upon on oath."[3]

Chrysippus, therefore, like Cleanthus, insists that *epiorkos* must be restricted only to the promissory oath, because a proposition concerning the future is true or false not objectively (*alethes* or *pseudes*), but subjectively (*euorkon* or *epiorkon*) only in the mind of the oath-taker; whereas a proposition concerning the past or present (an assertory oath) is an axiom, that is, true or false (*alethes* or *pseudes*) independently of the mind of the oath-taker, so that the man who, in good faith, swears falsely does not *epiorkein,* but simply *pseudorkei.*

Thus Aristotle, Cleanthus, and Chrysippus agree to the fact that the intention of the oath-taker is the essential factor of perjury; they disagree, however, as to whether the intention can be applied to the future (promissory oath) or the past and present (assertory oath).

Ethico-Religious Aspect of Perjury. In its religious aspect, perjury is directly connected with the curse of the oath. According to Homer (*Iliad* 23, 595), the perjurer is a sinner in the eyes of the gods, and the Furies (*Iliad* 3, 279) "under the earth take vengeance on men who have sworn a false oath." Even an unforeseen impossibility does not relieve one of the obligations of the oath. For instance, as has already been pointed out,[4] Hector, who promised on oath to give Achilles' horses to Dolon, is called perjurer (*epiorkon*) even though he was prevented from fulfilling his oath by Dolon's death. According to Hesiod (*Works and Days* 804), the perjurer turns the oath into a *pema* (punishment), and Hero-

3. *Ibid.* Cf. Diogenes Laertius, 7, 65-66. Cicero, *De Fato,* 20f and *De Officiis,* 3, 29.

4. *Iliad,* 10, 332.

dotus (6, 56) says that the perjurer is stricken by the curse (*toi agei enechetai*).

From these examples, one may argue that there was a belief that the formula of the curse had magic power, and that only fulfillment of the oath could break its spell. Not even the gods could escape the inevitability of the curse in case of perjury.[5] According to Herodotus (6, 86), Delphian Apollo assured that the curse would strike, if not the perjurer himself, then certainly his offspring.

Nonetheless, one must not forget that the Greeks considered the relationship between gods and men as contracts. Since, in contracts, bargaining was considered legitimate, so the clever wording of the oath-formula in order to ward off the divine punishment for perjury came to play a wide role. Homer (*Odyssey* 19, 396), for instance, praised Autolychus without reservation because he excelled other men in the art of deceitful oaths. Herodotus (4, 154) relates how "(Etearchus) befriended a man called Themiston from Thera . . . and obtained from him a promise upon oath to perform whatever service should be asked. Then, as soon as he had tendered the oath, he gave him his own daughter and told him to take her away and throw her into the sea. Themiston . . . put to sea with the girl . . . and, in order to clear himself of the obligation under which his oath had laid him, he lowered the girl into the water on the end of a rope and then hauled her up unharmed."

Thucydides reports how agreements were sometimes sworn under the stress of necessity and then broken at the next opportunity, and how the broken trust was considered as the prize of foresight (*xyneseos agonisma*).[6] Euripides,[7] too, argued that the gods knew how to separate forced oaths from voluntary oaths, and did not require their observance. Much quoted has been Euripides' statement in *Hyppolytus* (612) where the poet separates the proposition of the oath-formula from the intention of the oath-taker: "my tongue swore, not my mind."

The end result of this attitude was a form of *reservatio mentalis*, or intentionalism; the oath ceased to be a religious terror and became an ethical obligation, which could prove ineffectual when it came into conflict with higher duties. For instance, perjury, when it was required by the Fatherland, was considered just.

As a general rule, one may say that, until the end of the

5. Hesiod, *Theogony*, 782-806.

6. Thucydides, 3, 82-83.

7. Euripides, *Iphigeneia at Aulis*, 394a.

sixth century, divine punishment of perjury was still an effective deterrent against the misuse of the oath. From the fifth century, however, the individualism and relativism of the sophistic movement began to undermine the old notion of the oath, at least among a certain segment of the population, and fear of the gods, in case of perjury, began to wane. That is, the sophistic movement of the fifth century produced other categories of people, namely those who did not believe in the gods at all, those who believed that the gods existed but that they did not concern themselves with human affairs and, finally, those who believed it was not difficult to appease the gods' anger with gifts and sacrifices and thus buy off the merited punishment.

Lysander's[8] statement that children must be amused with dice and men with oaths may be regarded as the attitude of a large segment of the Greek élite. The proverbial Roman reference to "*Graeca Fides*" as synonymous with faithlessness was valid, with some reservations, not only for the Greeks with whom they had to deal, but also, *mutatis mutandis*, for the fifth-, fourth- and third-century Greeks. The Athenians, in fact, made a point of distinguishing their Attic faith (*attike pistis*) from the *pistis* of other Greeks.[9] A fragment of Xenophanes[10] points out how dissimilar was the burden of administering the oath to pious persons from that of administering it to unbelievers.

The philosophers, especially the Pythagoreans, waged a relentless war against the use of the oath. Pythagoras, for instance, used to warn his followers "rarely to take an oath, but once they had done so, by all means to stand by it."[11] According to Iamblicus,[12] Pythagoras also taught his followers rather to lose a case than to win it by an oath. A similar advice was given by Isocrates,[13] and the poet Sophocles (*Oedipus at Colonus* 650-1) wrote:

8. Plutarch, *Lysander*, 8, 3.

9. W. H. Roscher, "Pistis," *Lexikon der Griechischen und Römischen Mythologie* (Leipzig, 1902-1909). In respect to the Athenian temple to *Pistis*, it is difficult to decide whether it was built truly to the *Attike Pistis* or to the *Fides Romana*, since there is no trace of pre-Roman worship of *Pistis* among the Greeks, despite the fact that Theognis (1137) calls it *megale theos*. The Greeks, in fact, had always identified *Pistis* with *Themis* or *Dike* (Justice), and sometimes with Zeus, the guardian of oaths; hence, the epithets: *Zeus pistios*, *horkios* and *enorkios*. Cf. J. A. Hild, "Fides," *Darem.-Saglio*.

10. Aristotle, *Rhetoric*, 1, 15.

11. Diodorus, 10, 9, 2.

12. Iamblicus, *Pythagoras*, 47; cf. 144, 150.

13. Isocrates, *Demonicus*, 23.

"I'll not bind you by oath as though you were untrustworthy.
You'd get no more assurance than my word."

Socrates swore by the dog or the beech tree; the Athenian Lampon[14] swore by the goose; the philosopher Zeno swore by the goat in order to avoid swearing by the gods; and Menander (frag. 441) warns his audience: "Avoid swearing both for a good as well as a bad cause."

At the same time, mystical religions such as Orpheism and Pythagoreanism brought to philosophy a deeper interpretation of perjury. The perjurer must appease the divinity not simply by external sacrifices, but especially by personal atonement, spiritual conversion. The new religions, furthermore, emphasized the concept that the divinity sees not only the deeds, but also the thoughts of men.

In the Hellenistic period, the ruler-god was visible to the perjurer of the oath by the king (*basilikos horkos*), and the punishment was legal.[15] During the Empire, perjury of the oath by the *Genius* of the Emperor was a crime of *laesa majestas*.[16]

THE LEGAL ASPECT OF PERJURY. Perjury as an invocation to the gods to guarantee the truth of a false statement was a personal affront to the gods which carried its own penalty, the curse. There was no reason for an additional penalty by the state, and there are no records of a criminal action against perjury (*graphe epiorkias*); "(if) the person who has sworn . . . is proven not to have spoken the truth," says Demosthenes (23, 68), "he will bring the curse upon his children and his family, and this is all he would gain by it."

Perjury as false testimony was also a social breach and, consequently, a legal offense and subject to legal action. Such actions (criminal and civil actions) against false testimony (*graphai* and *dikai pseudomartyrion*) covered all kinds of false evidence, including cases of inheritance (*diamartyria*).[17]

According to Aristotle (*Politics* 1274b), Charondas was the first to institute the practice of denunciation for false witness. In Athens, the earliest information about actions against perjury as false testimony is given by Aristophanes (*Wasps* 782), Antiphon

14. Suidas, "Lampon," *Lexicon*.
15. Diodorus, 1, 77, 2.
16. Tacitus, *Ann.* 1, 73.
17. Dem. 24, 131; 29; 41, 16; 44; 45; 46; 47; 49, 56.

(5, 95), and Andocides (1, 7 and 74). It may be safe, at least for Athens, to date the legislation on perjury in the fifth century. Since however, at this time, depositions were generally oral,[18] cases of perjury must have been rare, because of the difficulty, inherent in oral evidence, of proving them. From the beginning of the fourth century, when all depositions became written, perjury cases were more frequent, since they were easier to prove.[19]

By Demosthenes' time, notice for perjury had to be given before the judges voted. Such a notice was called *episkepsis*.[20] In cases of inheritance (*diamartyria*), the *episkepsis* suspended the principal case until the trial for false testimony (*pseudomartyrion dike*) was concluded. In all other cases the *episkepsis* did not suspend the original trial, but in cases involving death, exile, or loss of citizenship, it produced a stay of execution of the sentence until the conclusion of the trial for false testimony (*pseudomartyrion dike*).[21] In cases involving a small fine, there was probably no delay in execution.

According to Demosthenes (47, 2), prosecution for false testimony was encouraged by law, which imposed only a slight penalty on the prosecutor in cases of failure, and in certain cases permitted the retrial of the original case: "For this reason they have decreed a smaller penalty for the plaintiff if he loses the case, in order that those who have been wronged may not be deterred by a heavy fine from prosecuting witnesses for false testimony, but they have imposed heavy penalties upon the defendant, if he is convicted and thought by you to have given false testimony."

Technically, the *episkepsis* was not the same as the *dike pseudomartyrion*. The former was simply a notice given at the trial to impeach a certain testimony; the latter was the formal indictment, and the trial itself, of false evidence. There was no heavy penalty but the forfeiture of a small fee, in case the party that brought forth the *episkepsis* failed to follow it up with the formal indictment of *dike pseudomartyrion*. So sometimes it was expedient, according to Demosthenes (47, 49), to introduce only the *episkep-*

18. G. M. Calhoun, "Oral and Written Pleadings in Athenian Courts," *APAT*, 50 (1919).

19. The most famous case is that of Isocrates' dead woman (18, 52-54). Almost as famous is that of Dem. 48, 44.

20. Dem. 48, 44f; 52, 28.

21. Dem. 24, 131. On the other hand, for the fifth-century procedure see Antiphon 5, 95, and Andocides 1, 7 and 74.

sis against some important testimony in order to offset its weight in the minds of the judges.

According to Demosthenes (34, 19), again, no punishment was provided for those who gave false testimony before arbitrators: "For it is not the same, men of Athens, to give false evidence before you and before the arbitrator; great indignation and penalty await those who gave false testimony before you; but before the arbitrator they give what evidence they wish, without risk and without shame." Therefore, from these passages it appears that there was a provision for prosecutors of false testimony in cases before the popular courts.[22]

The penalty imposed on a convicted witness was determined by the judges. In a private action *(dike pseudomartyrion)*, it was a fine, probably paid to the wronged party. In a public action *(graphe pseudomartyrion)*, the penalty was probably divided up into a compensation paid to the prosecutor and a punitive fine paid to the treasury. Furthermore, according to Demosthenes (29, 16), the false witness was liable to a charge of contempt of court, with the penalty of loss of citizenship rights (*atimia*). "In the second place, [Aesius] would not have been silent, but would have sued me for damages, if I had made him accountable to a charge of false testimony against his brother, a charge on which men run the risk both of a fine and of *atimia*." However, it is not certain whether the *atimia* was inflicted after a second or third conviction of perjury.[23]

Demosthenes[24] also says that a party who produced a false witness could be sued for subornation *(dike kakotechnion)*, but he gives no information about the penalty. There is no example of a case of *dike kakotechnion*.

In Stymphalos[25] the unsuccessful plaintiff, failing to get at least one third of the votes, had to pay to the alleged perjurer an amount equivalent to one third of the litigation sum. On the other hand, a witness convicted of perjury had to pay the damages done to the wronged person, the same, probably, as in Athens, plus a fine as a punitive penalty for false testimony. In Locri[26] the perjurer had

22. Cf. Dem. 34, 46. See also G. M. Calhoun, "Perjury before Athenian Arbitrators," *CP*, 10 (1915).

23. Andocides, 1, 74.

24. Dem. 46, 10; 47, 1; 49, 56.

25. Schwyzer, *op. cit.*, no. 668.

26. Schwyzer, *op. cit.*, no. 366.

to pay in *duplum*. Finally, in Egypt (*Halle papyrus*), when the successful trial of a perjurer suspended the judgment of the principal trial, the punishment for the perjurer was one and a half times the litigation sum, payable to the state.

CONCLUSION. One can conclude from the foregoing survey that perjury, as an ethico-religious offense, was a matter left entirely to the gods or to the conscience of the individuals, some of whom did not hesitate to use the oath unscrupulously, whereas perjury, as false testimony, was a legal offence and subject to a fine in order to compensate for the wrong done.

It may also be concluded that there was a certain development in the legal punishment for perjury, showing a gradual progression from simple compensation to the wronged person to an additional, punitive fine to be paid to the state.

SEVEN

Conclusion

Some legal historians, Sir H. S. Maine in particular, claim that society evolved from status stage to contract stage, and the link was constituted by the promissory oath.

In the status stage the individual was not yet considered as a legal person. He acted as a member of a family or a class, which was actually the legal atom. Since the individual did not have any decision-making capacity, he lacked, consequently, individual responsibility. His family, his class, or his community accounted for his actions: the whole, through its representative leader, jealously answered for its integral parts. The members of early commonwealths, in fact, considered or assumed themselves to be of a common lineage. They were bound together socially, religiously, and by kinship through the legal fiction of adoption. The individuals of such communities were anonymous entities and tended to become partisans of their members against outsiders. Consequently, they also tended to rely on force (*bia, vis*) in settling disputes rather than on negotiations or even arbitration.

In the status stage, furthermore, social conscience was still very young. Its ethical principles were still in the process of development and its (customary) laws, which are believed to represent mankind's effort toward self-domestication, were still scanty and of primitive and archaic quality. In the Homeric epic, for instance, the deceitful cunning of Ulysses appears as a virtue on the same rank with the wisdom of Nestor, the courage of Hector, and the prowess of Achilles. Finally, it must be noted that the moral growth of social conscience is subordinate to the social needs of the times.

At this early level of development the social system was based on the principle of strict reciprocity—*do ut des*— (I give you that you may give me) or an eye for an eye and a tooth for a tooth. Such a reciprocity was real and immediate. Young societies, in fact, do not fully understand the nature of moral obligation or responsibility. Promises of sales, for instance, were not binding. Sales were on a *hic et nunc* (here and now) basis; they were not founded on promises (future obligations), but on the actual transfer of property (present obligation), and it was of no importance whether the transactions were honest or fraudulent, free or under duress. The relatives of an injured or murdered man, acting as partisans, were not concerned with the responsibility of the incident, but rather with reprisal. The blood curse, furthermore, did not strike only the murderer, but his whole family. Customary law was primarily a law of wrongs, of delicts, based on the principle of vengeance, of *lex talionis* (strict justice).

The nature of obligation was fully understood when the individual person was morally emancipated from his family or community, with which he was identified entirely, and was declared a legal person *per se*. This actually happened when the doctrine of individual equality before the law was firmly established. Now the individual, and the individual alone, became accountable for his actions; he was now recognized as capable of making decisions and, consequently, being responsible for them. The blood curse, for instance, no longer extended to the whole family, but was now restricted to the individual murderer, that is, there was a development from family curse to personal curse.

With the recognition of individual moral responsibility the full development of the concept of contract was reached. The moral freedom of the individual implied also freedom of contract, whereby the individual was given almost unlimited permission to make promises. Mankind thus reached social maturity; its law became now primarily a law of obligation derived from the agreements of the individuals.

Legal historians also claim that the transitional stage from status to contract was constituted by the institutions of surety and pledge. The surety at first was a hostage who in case of default was treated with the harshness that would have been meted out to the debtor. A defaulting debtor was thought of not merely as a breaker of promises, but as a thief, and, consequently, subject to the harsh laws of delict. Later, the surety merely promised that he would pay the loan, if the debtor did not. The surety, obviously, in his turn, relied on the promise of the debtor that he would pay.

The pledge at first was regarded as forfeit, that is, in case the debtor failed to pay the debt on the appointed day, the creditor was entitled to retain possession of the pledged object, regardless of its value. In a sense, the pledge was still a form of barter, still associated with the ancient possessory ideas, because, though initially the pledged object was not the basis of the transaction, it became such in case of default.

In these early stages, therefore, of the development of the law the creditor asked for something tangible which would serve as security for the performance of the duty by the debtor; he wanted to have actually in his power some person (i.e., a hostage) or something (i.e., a pledge), who or which would be liable or forfeit in case his rights were not safeguarded.

But the most popular institution for the ultimate origin of the contract is considered to have been the promissory oath, whereby one promised to repay a loan or to pay a settlement in order to avoid a blood-feud. The promissory oath was thus an inchoate contract. In fact, here was a true case of future obligation. This obligation, however, was not directly between the parties concerned, but through the god (or gods) invoked in the oath. God acted here not only as a witness of the debtor's or delinquent's promise, but, most important of all as a surety of it. By this divine intervention the human hostage was removed, because the creditor accepted now the guarantee of the oath-god. He (the creditor) was relying, therefore, not on the *pistis* (faith) of the debtor, but on the magical power of the oath-formula, namely, the curse to assure the performance of the debtor. But, though at first failure to keep the oath was punishable only by the curse, later it was treated as crime, because the cursed person was believed to pollute and, therefore, to endanger the whole community. Thus, the concept of dual punishment—the religious (the curse), which was left entirely to the vengeance of the gods, and the political, which was carried out by the state—came into existence. This concept of dual punishment implied a kind of separation between religion and politics, an incipient secular administration of justice, in brief, the secularization of the state.

In the process of this evolution of society from status to contract the rise of the state authority obviously played a very important role.

In the unsettled stage of the Mycenaean world and the early Dorian period, when might still made right, men often solved their disputes by the might of the club. So, too, did the gods, who were made in the image of men: "I am your king," was the challenge of Zeus before the assembly of the gods in the *Iliad*, "because I am the strongest of all." Indeed, the Homeric epic, namely the *Iliad*, is, to some extent, the glorification of might.

In this early stage of the evolution of mankind, the regulation of life and the administration of justice within the clan-family were functions exercised predominantly by the clan-chiefs. Disputes between clans of the same community were mostly dealt with by the clans concerned. These could solve their quarrels by recourse to force, to negotiation, or even to arbitration by the king or the elders of the community. Disputes with members outside the community, however, would concern the whole community under the leadership of the king. It usually meant war.

When the Greek invaders had, at last, settled down, notions of rights of real property were developed and the rudiments of social justice were evolved from the social instinct of man through the needs created by the new social conditions. There appeared now a semblance of social order, an incipient *kosmos*. Zeus ceased to be the boorish ruler whose authority (*kratos*) rested exclusively on force (*bia*), and became the father of justice and the avenger of wrong-doers. Thus, religion appeared as the legitimate authority to enforce justice among the clans of the community, to tame the violent nature of young mankind. Self-help and reprisals were now controlled by an appeal to divine justice. Alongside the sheer assertion of force (*bia*), we now witness also the religious challenge—the religious duel, the ordeal, and the decisory oath (*proklesis eis horkon*). In the more ancient legislations, as for instance in that of Gortyn, one party was allowed to take such an oath; in general, the defendant was the *horkioteros* (the more suitable to take the oath).

At last, man had submitted to arbitration. As a matter of precaution, however, the arbitrator could not yet be a fellow man, because he was not yet believed capable of being above partisanship in the disputes. Once the conscience of early people had matured this far, to wit, to accepting the principle of divine appeal, then the necessary step was the establishment of public authority as an emanation from god.

But when the authority of the community, invested in the king, claimed to derive its legitimacy from the divine power, to be the intermediate agent of god, then the king claimed the right to interfere in the internal life of the clans, not only in the quarrels among the clans of the community, but also in the internal matters of the clan itself. This intrusion, however, brought a clash between the centralizing forces, polarized around the king, and the decentralizing ones, entrenched in the traditional sovereign powers of the clans. The struggle ended with the supremacy of the community-authority in the hands, however, not of the king, but of the clan-chiefs, and the archaic age was thus ushered in.

The decisive confrontation, obviously, was caused by the administration of justice and the enforcement of its decisions. These judicial decisions given by an incipient public authority (first by the king and the elders of the community, later by the magistrates) in time grew into a body of precedents that eventually constituted the customs or customary law (*ta patria, mos majorum*) of the community.

This assertion of public authority in turn brought about a change in the relationship among the members of the community: by incorporating the clans into the state structure, the state assured for itself the allegiance of the individuals. This meant that the individual was to some extent emancipated from his clan and attached to the state. Whereas, before, the individual rallied his clan in whatever serious disputes he might have been involved, he now *could* refer (voluntary arbitration) and later *must* refer (compulsory arbitration) the matter to the state.

Now society was ready for formal legislation. This came with the first codes, which were not mere codifications of the customary laws, but also alterations and emendations of them. The archaic codes had thus a distinctly innovating character. The sanction of the customary laws, for instance, was primarily religious and social (*aidos*), whereas the sanction of the codes was also political. Thus, the community evolved from self-help to compulsory arbitration and legislation. The state was now in the saddle.

The authority of the state, however, was still supported by the gods of the community, and the oath remained an essential part of the arbitration procedure. But now it had lost its decisory power before the magistrate-judge. The gods would now manifest their will not directly, but through the magistrate duly appointed by the community. Both parties now took the oath, but the magistrate-judge would decide who swore rightly (*poteros euorkei*).

The formula *poteros euorkei*, elaborated at the time of Solon, emptied the oath of its decisory power in court. Until then, the oath constituted both the proof and the decision, i.e., the whole trial. Now it was still part of the legal procedure, but it no longer formed the decision in law-courts. This had been separated from the means of proof and entrusted to the magistrate-judge. The judge, in his turn, though he might claim some religious charisma in the exercise of his functions, now received his power, his investiture, not directly from the state-gods but from the people, and the mutual oath—of the people to obey, and of the judge to respect the laws—formed the constitutional basis of his power.

With the institution of the magistrate-judge directly responsible to the community, the official religion began to lose its absolute ascendancy over the community. Thus, the basis for the separation of the political authority from religion was established. The community had reached the threshold of maturity. In fact, it began now to seek another source for the administration of justice, to wit, the conscience of the judge, and the road for the rationalization of justice was thus opened. However, it must be noted that the decisory oath was still permitted before the magistrate-judge in the preliminary hearings and before both the public and private arbitrators. But by the fourth century B.C. it was very rarely used even in these situations.

The history of Greek institutions thus fell approximately into three periods: in the first, the community was composed of clan-families which jealously guarded their internal sovereignty and subordinated all their members to their own common good; in the second, the clan-families surrendered their internal sovereignty to the community and the polis thus was born; in the third, the individuals asserted their moral freedom before the polis, which thus lost its all-pervading nature and in practice came to control only the political aspect of society. Obviously, such social and political evolution was to a certain degree correlated to the economic evolution.

Until the end of the eighth century, in fact, the Greek communities had no resources worth speaking of except agriculture and stock breeding. Their social structures were, to some extent, patriarchal and static. But now a great age of colonization began. Commerce and trade on a relatively large scale developed. Work shops and markets soon appeared throughout the Aegean sea and all around the Black sea. In the west the major trading centers appeared in southern Italy. The introduction of money, of course, was instrumental in such an economic revolution.

The economic awakening had in turn strong repercussions in the social and political system. It can best be seen by contrasting the commercial communities, such as Miletus, Corinth, Athens and others which developed into great urban centers, displaying a mobile and individualistic life, with the agricultural-pastoral communities, such as Achaea, Aetolia, Phocis, Boeotia, and others which remained in a rural stage with clannish customs and static life. Most important of all, the introduction of money and the new sources of revenue, based on trade and commerce, started the process of emancipation of the individual. And economic individualism was thus now on its way. Maybe, Alcaeus (frag. 49) was not entirely wrong when he said that money makes the man. A man in debt, for instance, who was unable to pay his loan at the appointed day, was generally seized as late as Solon's age and sold into slavery or reduced to the status of a serf. Thus, just as poverty was the beginning of servitude, so money was of freedom.

The new economic atmosphere and the development of the concept of contract were obviously closely associated with the evolution of the concept of property. This we believe is best illustrated by the concept of *kleros* (estate). At first the *kleros* was considered inalienable and common property of the whole clan. The clan-leader was merely the official administrator of it. In time, however, the right of administration was transformed into a right of ownership at the family level. This actually happened when, at the time of Solon, wills were officially recognized. By such a recognition the head of the family could will his portion of the *kleros* to people originally outside his clan through the legal fiction of adoption. Later, according to J. V. A. Fine, from the end of the fifth century, the householder, probably with the consent of the family, could mortgage it with a right of redemption, a right which more often than not remained unclaimed. In short, the *kleros* was preserved as long as the family unity and the belief in its perpetuation was strong. But as soon as the concept of the historical identity of the family was undermined (first, by Solon's testamentary adoption; then, by the double invasion of the Persians; finally, by the catastrophic effects of the Peloponnesian war, especially by the immigration of the rural population into the city and the subsequent plague), the *kleros* lost the *raison d'être* of its inalienability. Then, it was no longer a question of principle, but a question of practice and time that *de facto* made the *kleros* alienable and the concept of personal property was extended also to immovables. The inalienability of the *kleros*, however, always remained subordinate first to the tribal community and then to the polis. The polis in fact occasionally did confiscate *kleroi* and redistribute them.[1]

We started this monograph by analyzing the nature of the oath. It was determined that a definition of the oath which would apply to the ancient Greek world had to include the following three elements: (1) a solemn declaration of the truth (assertory oath) or of promise (promissory oath); (2) an invocation of a local god or gods to guarantee such a declaration; and (3) a religious sanction in the form of a curse, in case the person taking the oath perjured himself.

The next step was to examine the applications of the oath in the various aspects of life.

In public law we saw that the legitimacy of a child, which also determined his future religious and political standing, was confirmed by the sworn declaration of the father; that registration in the citizen roll was preceded by a religious, political and military oath, whereby the candidate pledged his loyalty to the gods, laws, and safety of the state; that a new constitution (democratic, oligarchic, monarchic, or tyrannic) also demanded a loyalty oath from all citizens in order to guarantee a certain harmony (*homonoia*) among the factions of the state (thus was affirmed the principle

1. Cf. Sir Paul Vinogradoff, *op. cit.*, p. 202; J. V. A. Fine, *Horoi* (Baltimore, 1951), pp. 167 ff.

of separation between constitution and state); that the citizens were sometimes required to ratify treaties, public contracts, and new laws by oath, so as to be individually responsible for these ratifications; that the refusal to take the oath could result in partial or total loss of citizenship (*atimia*); that all public officials had to take a promissory oath before entering office; and, finally, that any citizen who wanted to decline political appointments, military duty, even taxation, could do so by a reasonable excuse, corroborated by an exemption oath (*exomosia*).

It was, however, in judicial life that we were able to see, through the process of the secularization of the administration of justice, the evolution from the decisory oath to the mere procedural oath, from divine justice to state justice.

The magistrate-judges, like the other public officials—fully or partially employed—were required to take the promissory oath when they entered on their office, except that in some early legislation, as for instance in that of Gortyn, they were sometimes bound to pass judgment on oath, like the kings and the elders in early times. The public arbitrators, like the magistrate-judges, were also subject to the promissory oath whenever they were called to give judgment. The private arbitrators, however, were not bound by law to take such an oath, and generally they tried to persuade the parties to a mutual agreement without having to pass judgment. But any time they had to give sentence, the parties usually asked them to give it on oath. Obviously, the function of the oath in such cases was to guarantee to the parties the impartiality of their decision.

The litigants themselves always took the declaratory oath in the preliminary hearings before the thesmothetai to attest the sincerity of their claims. However, they could still solve their dispute by appeal to the decisory oath in the preliminary hearings and before the arbitrator, but this was very rarely done, as mentioned above.

In regard to the oath of the witnesses, we saw that in civil cases the oath became voluntary, but in homicide cases it was still obligatory; the testimony, however, always remained obligatory. The legal dictum was: testify or take the oath (*martyrein e exomnysthai*). In case the witness refused to do either, he was fined, according to Aeschines, one thousand drachmae.

The oath continued to constitute the juridical basis of treaties among states, but its value as a deterrent against violators became more and more a formality. In international arbitration, as in internal judicial procedure, the oath was a *condicio sine qua non*: judges, litigants and witnesses each had to take his respective oath.

In social life the oath preserved, in some instances, its magical, religious force, as in conspiracies or other illicit activities.

Finally, dealing with the question of perjury, we saw how the secularization of the law brought about the distinction between sworn statement or testimony corroborated by oath and oath proper or curse. Perjury as an affront to the deities (*epiorkia*) invoked in the oath had its own penalty (the curse), the execution of which was a matter left entirely to the power of the gods (*deorum iniurias dis curae*). Perjury as false testimony was subject to legal action (*dike pseudomartyrion*). As such it raised two questions: (a) what was the effect of a perjury conviction on the original trial, and (b) what was the penalty inflicted upon the perjurer.

To the first question there is no clear answer. From Demosthenes and Isaeus it appears that in civil cases the conviction of a single witness was sufficient cause for a retrial of the original suit. However, in homicide cases, according to Antiphon, Andocides and Lysias, the conviction of a witness as a perjurer might come too late to affect the death sentence of the original trial. However, sometime during the fourth century B.C., a law was passed decreeing that in homicide cases the *episkepsis* should produce a stay of execution of the sentence until the conclusion of the *dike pseudomartyrion*. In all other cases, such a stay was not necessary, because the injured party could recover, in a subsequent trial, all damages done to him by the perjurer.

To the second question also the answer is not clear. It appears from the orators that for the first offense of perjury the penalty was a fine, but for two or more convictions the penalty was a fine plus partial *atimia*.

In brief, the oath in ancient Greece was used:

1. As a contract. This was the case of the promissory oath: the oath-taker solemnly engaged himself to abide by the conditions stipulated in the oath.

2. As decisive evidence. As such it determined both the private settlement of disputes by the litigants themselves and the decisions of the arbitrators when they were called upon, but it is very doubtful whether it was *de iure* peremptory on the dicasts,

although there can be little doubt that *de facto* the latter were influenced by the *proklesis eis horkon.*

3. As a means of evidence. As such it corroborated the truth of a statement, as in the case of the disclaimer oath. Such an oath was accepted before the dicasts, but its probative power derived not from the legal, but the religious sanction, the curse. The law punished only false testimony.

4. As a form of attestation to the sincerity of the litigants in stating their claims. The oath here was merely declaratory. It had no legal, but only religious sanction.

Therefore, in courts of law, Athens, at least, had almost reached the end of the road in the evolution and secularization of the oath, from the magical, religious stage, in which the oath was believed to act *ex opere operato,* to a more or less solemn formality of trial procedure. And the major turning point was made when the Sophists separated *nomos* (law) from *physis* (nature). The *nomoi,* then, ceased to be religious precepts and became juridical paragraphs in the new rational systematization of the laws, carried out at the end of the fifth century in Athens. The secularization was now almost complete, and the official religion became simply a venerable institution.

The state-authority practically had almost disengaged itself from religion and began to act on its own right. Consequently, it had to seek a new basis of justice, which it hoped to find in human reason, specifically in the conscience of the judge, and to limit its coercive function to the enforcement of the state justice, whereas the gods themselves became now responsible for the enforcement of their rights.

Socrates seems to have embodied, in his tragic end, this spiritual crisis caused by the transition between the old religious and political concept of the all-pervading polis and the new moral freedom of the individual, that is, on one hand, his unconditional identification with the polis, on the other, his moral autonomy before it. Thus, he was not so much the victim of human blindness, as, especially, the victim of the conflict of these two forces present also in himself.

Bibliography

Adler, A., ed. *Lexicographi Graeci*. 5 vols. Leipzig, 1929-38.

Aeschines. *Orationes*, ed. F. Blass. Leipzig, 1908.

Aeschylus. *Aeschyli Tragoediae*, ed. G. Murray. Oxford, 1937.

Andocides. *Orationes*, ed. Blass-Fuhr. Leipzig, 1913.

Antiphon. *Orationes*, ed. Blass-Thalheim. Leipzig, 1914.

Aristophanes. *Aristophanis Comoediae*, eds. F. W. Hall and W. M. Geldart. 2nd ed. 2 vols. Oxford, 1906-7.

Aristotle. *Constitution of Athens*, ed. F. G. Kenyon. Oxford, 1920.

————. *Politics*, ed. W. D. Ross. Oxford, 1957.

————. *The Politics of Aristotle*, trans. E. Barker. Oxford, 1948.

————. *Rhetoric*, ed. W. D. Ross. Oxford, 1959.

Bekker, I., ed. *Lexica Segueriana* in *Anecdota Graeca*. Berlin, 1814-21.

Berneker, E. "Pseudomartyrion Dike," *RE*, XLVI (1959), 1362-1385.

Black, H. C. *Law Dictionary*. 4th ed. St. Paul, Minn., 1951.

Blass, F. *Die Attische Beredsamkeit*. 2nd ed. 3 vols. Leipzig, 1887-98 (Rp. by Olms/Hildesheim, 1962).

Boisacq, E. *Dictionnaire Étymologique de la Langue Grecque*. 4th ed. Heidelberg, 1950.

Bonner, R. J. "Apollodorus *vs* Phormio; criminal assault," *CP*, vol. 14 (1919), pp. 83-84.

————. *Evidence in Athenian Courts*. Chicago, 1905.

————. "Evidence in the Areopagus," *CP*, vol. 7 (1912), pp. 450-56.

————. "The Institution of Athenian Arbitrators," *CP*, vol. 11 (1916), pp. 191-95.

Bonner, R. J. "The Jurisdiction of Athenian Arbitrators," *CP*, vol. 2 (1907), pp. 407-18.

Bonner, R. J., and G. Smith. *The Administration of Justice from Homer to Aristotle*. 2 vols. Chicago, 1930-38.

———. "Administration of Justice in Sparta," *CP*, vol. 37 (1942), pp. 113-29.

———. "Administration of Justice in the Delphic Amphictyony," *CP*, vol. 38 (1943), pp. 1-12.

———. "Administration of Justice in Boeotia," *CP*, vol. 40 (1945), pp. 11-23.

Botsford, G. W. "Development of the Athenian Constitution," *CSCP*, no. 4, 1893.

Botsford, G. W., and E. G. Sihler. *Hellenic Civilization*. New York, 1915.

Buck, C. D. *The Greek Dialects*. Rev. ed. Chicago, 1955.

Busolt, G., and H. Swoboda. *Griechische Staatskunde*. 2 vols. (In I. von Mueller's *Handbuch*). Munich, 1920-26.

Butcher, S. H., and W. Rennie. *Demosthenis Orationes*. 3 vols. Oxford, 1903-31.

Caillemer, E. "Amphiorkia," "Anakrisis," and "Diomosia," *Darem.-Saglio*.

Caimo, I. "Il Giuramento nell'Arbitrato Convenzionale in Diritto Attico," *Studi Italiani di Filologia Classica*, n.s. vol. 5 (1927), pp. 15-26.

Calabi, I. *Ricerche sui Rapporti fra le Poleis*. Firenze, 1953.

Calhoun, G. M. *Athenian Clubs in Politics and Litigation*. Austin, 1913.

———. "Athenian Magistrates and Special Pleas," *CP*, vol. 14 (1919), pp. 338-50.

———. "Demosthenes against Boeotus," *CP*, vol. 16 (1921), pp. 287-88.

———. "Diamartyria, Paragraphe and the Law of Archinus," *CP*, vol. 13 (1918), pp. 169-85.

———. "Documentary Frauds in Litigation at Athens," *CP*, vol. 9 (1914), pp. 134-44.

———. "Episkepsis and the Dike Pseudomartyrion," *CP*, vol. 11 (1916), pp. 365-94.

———. "Oral and Written Pleading in Athenian Courts," *APAT*, vol. 50 (1919), pp. 177-93.

———. "Paragraphe and Arbitration," *CP*, vol. 14 (1919), pp. 20-28.

———. "Perjury before Athenian Arbitrators," *CP*, vol 10 (1915), pp. 1-7.

Calhoun, G. M., and C. Delamere. *A Working Bibliography of Greek Law*. Cambridge, Mass., 1927.

Cicero. *De Fato*, ed. and trans. A. Yon. Paris, 1944.

———. *De Officiis*, ed. E. P. Crowell. 2nd ed. Philadelphia, 1882.

Cronin, J. F. *The Athenian Juror and his Oath*. Chicago, 1936 (diss.).

Daremberg, C., and E. Saglio, eds. *Dictionnaire des Antiquités Grecques et Romaines d'après les textes et les Monuments*. Paris, 1877-1919.

Dareste, R., B. Haussoullier, and Th. Reinach. *Recueil des Inscriptions Juridiques Grecques*. Ser. 1-2. Paris, 1895-1904.

Demosthenes. *Démosthène, Plaidoyers Civils*, ed. L. Gernet. 4 vols. Paris, 1954-60.

———. *Démosthène, Plaidoyers Politiques*, ed. L. Gernet, J. Humbert, G. Matthieu, O. Navarre, and P. Orsini. 4 vols. Paris, 1945-59.

———. *The Orations of Demosthenes*, trans. C. R. Kennedy. 5 vols. London, 1880-81.

Diodorus Siculus. *The Bibliotheca Historica*, ed. and trans. C. H. Oldfather *et alii*. 12 vols. Cambridge, Mass., 1939-67.

Diogenes Laertius. *Vitae Philosophorum*, ed. H. S. Long. 2 vols. Oxford, 1964.

Dittenberger, W. *Sylloge Inscriptionum Graecarum*. 3rd ed. Leipzig, 1915 (Rp. by Olms/Hildesheim, 1960).

Dorjahn, A. P. *Political Forgiveness in Old Athens.* Evanston, Ill., 1946.
———. "On the Athenian Anakrisis," *CP,* vol. 36 (1941), pp. 182-85.
Ehrenberg, V. *The Greek State.* New York, 1960.
———. *Aspects of the Ancient World.* New York, 1946.
Euripides. *Euripidis Tragoediae,* ed. G. Murray. 3 vols. Oxford, 1901-13.
Forman, L. L. *Index Andocideus, Lycurgeus, Dinarcheus.* Oxford, 1897.
Fustel de Coulanges, N. D. *La Cité Antique.* 22nd ed. Paris, 1912.
Gernet, L. *Droit et Société dans la Grèce Ancienne.* Paris, 1964.
Glotz, G. "Jusjurandum" and "Proklesis," *Darem.-Saglio.*
———. *The Greek City,* trans. N. Mallinson. New York, 1930.
———. *Ancient Greece at Work,* trans. M. R. Dobie. New York, 1927.
Glotz, G., and R. Cohen. *Histoire Grecque.* 4th ed. 2 vols. Paris, 1948.
Greenidge, A. J. H. *A Handbook of Greek Constitutional History.* Oxford, 1920.
Grotius, H. *De Iure Belli et Pacis,* bk. 2, ch. 13.
Hager, H. "Theophrastus' peri nomon," *JP,* vol. 6 (1876), pp. 1-27.
Harrison, A. R. W. *The Law of Athens.* Oxford, 1968.
Harpocration. *Lexicon in Decem Oratores Atticos,* ex recensione G. Dindorfii. Oxford, 1854.
Haussoullier, B. "Epiorkia," *Darem.-Saglio.*
Headlam, J. W. "The Procedure of the Gortynian Inscription," *JHS,* vol. 13 (1892-93), pp. 48-69.
———. "On the Proklesis eis Basanon in Attic Law," *CR,* vol. 7 (1893), pp. 1-5.
Herodotus. *Herodoti Historiae,* ed. C. Hude. 3rd ed. 2 vols. Oxford, 1927.
Hesiod. *Hesiodi Carmina,* ed. A. Rzach. 3rd cd. Leipzig, 1913.
Hesychius Alexandrinus. *Lexicon,* ex recensione M. Schmidt. 5 vols. Jena, 1858-68.
Hignett, C. *A History of the Athenian Constitution.* Oxford, rp. 1962.
Hirzel, R. *Der Eid.* Leipzig, 1902.
———. *Themis, Dike und Verwandtes.* Leipzig, 1907.
Hofmann, G. *De Jurejurandi apud Athenienses Formulis.* Darmstadt, 1886 (diss.).
Holmes, D. H. *Index Lysiacus.* Bonn, 1895.
Homer. *Homeri opera,* eds. D. B. Monro and T. W. Allen. 5 vols. Oxford, 1911-20.
Iamblicus. *De vita Pythagorica,* ed. L. Deubner. Leipzig, 1937.
Isaeus. *Speeches,* ed. W. Wyse. Cambridge, Eng., 1904.
Isocrates. *Orationes,* ed. F. Blass. 2 vols. Leipzig, 1895-99.
Jolowicz, H. F. *Historical Introduction to the Study of Roman Law.* 2nd ed. Cambridge, Eng., 1952 (Rp. with corrections, 1961).
Jones, A. H. *The Athens of Demosthenes.* Cambridge, Eng., 1952.
Jones, J. W. *Law and Legal Theory of the Greeks.* Oxford, 1956.
Kirk, G. S., and J. E. Raven, eds. *The Presocratic Philosophers.* Cambridge, Eng., 1960.
Lämmli, F. *Das Attische Prozessverfahren in seiner Wirkung auf die Gerichtsrede.* Paderborn, 1938.
Latte, K. "Meineid," *RE.*
Leutsch, E. L. A., and F. G. Schneidewin, eds. *Paroemiographi Graeci.* 2 vols. Göttingen, 1839-51.
Lipsius, J. *Das Attische Recht und Rechtsverfahren.* Leipzig, 1915.
Lycurgus. *Orationes,* ed. F. Blass. Leipzig, 1894.
Lysias. *Orationes,* ed. C. Hude. Oxford, 1913.
MacDowell, D. M. *Athenian Homicide Law.* Manchester, 1963.

MacDowell, D. M. *Andokides on the Mysteries.* Oxford, 1962.

Maine, H. S. *Ancient Law.* 10th ed. London, 1884 (Rp. by Beacon Press, Boston, 1963).

Mederle, C. *De Jurisjurandi in Lite Attica Decem Oratorum Aetate Usu.* Munich, 1902 (diss.).

Meiggs, R. "The Growth of Athenian Imperialism," *JHS,* vol. 63 (1943), pp. 21-34.

________. "A note on Athenian Imperialism," *CR,* vol. 63 (1949), pp. 9-12.

Michel, C. *Recueil d'Inscriptions Grecques.* 2 vols. Paris-Brussels, 1899-1927.

Murray, G. *Five Stages of Greek Religion.* Oxford, 1925.

Myres, J. L. *The Political Ideas of the Greeks.* New York, 1927.

Nicholas, B. *An Introduction to Roman Law.* Oxford, 1962.

Nilsson, M. P. *Geschichte der Griechischen Religion.* 2 vols. Munich, 1941-50.

________. *Cults, Myths, Oracles and Politics in Ancient Greece.* Lund, 1951.

Oliver, J. H. *Demokratia, the Gods and the Free World.* Baltimore, 1960.

Ott, L. *Beiträge zur Kentniss des Griechischen Eides.* Leipzig, 1896.

Paoli, U. E. *Studi sul Processo Attico.* Padua, 1933.

Pauly A., G. Wissowa, and W. Kroll, eds. *Real-Encyclopädie der Klassischen Altertumswissenschaft.* Stuttgart, 1893—.

Pausanias. *Pausanias' Description of Greece,* trans. and comm. J. G. Frazer. 2nd ed. 6 vols. London, 1913.

Perrot, G. *Essais sur le Droit Public et Privé de la République Athénienne.* Paris, 1867.

Phillipson, C. *The International Law and Customs of Ancient Greece and Rome.* 2 vols. London, 1911.

Plato. *Platonis opera,* ed. J. Burnet. 5 vols. Oxford, 1901-6.

________. *The Dialogues of Plato,* trans. B. Jowett. 4th ed. revised by D. J. Allan and H. E. Dale. 4 vols. Oxford, 1953.

Plutarch. *Moralia,* ed. G. N. Bernardakis. 7 vols. Leipzig, 1888-96.

________. *Vitae,* eds. C. Lindskog and K. Ziegler. 4 vols. Leipzig, 1914-35.

Pollux. *Onomasticon,* ed. C. W. Dindorf. 4 vols. Leipzig, 1824.

Polybius. *The Histories of Polybius,* trans. E. S. Shuckburgh. London, 1889.

Preuss, S. *Index Demosthenicus.* Leipzig, 1892.

________. *Index Aeschinius.* Leipzig, 1896.

Pufendorf, S. *De Iure Naturae et Gentis,* bk. 4, ch. 2.

Rohde, E. *Psyche,* trans. W. B. Hillis. New York, 1925.

Roscher, W. H. *Lexikon der Griechischen und Römischen Mythologie.* Leipzig, 1902-9.

Sartori, F. *Le Eterie nella Vita Politica Ateniese del VI e V Secolo avanti Cristo.* Roma, 1957.

Schaefer, A. D. *Demosthenes und seine Zeit.* 2nd ed. 3 vols. Leipzig, 1885-87.

Schoeman, G. F., and J. H. Lipsius. *Griechische Alterthümer.* 2 vols. Berlin, 1897-1902.

Schwyzer, E. *Dialectorum Graecarum Exempla Epigraphica Potiora.* Leipzig, 1923 (Rp. by Olms/Hildesheim, 1960).

Seagle, W. *The Quest for Law.* New York, 1941.

Sophocles. *Sophoclis Tragoediae,* ed. A. C. Pearson. Oxford, 1923.

Stobaeus. *Anthologium (Eclogae et Florilegium),* eds. C. Wachsmuth and O. Hense. 5 vols. Leipzig, 1884-1923.

Suidas. *Lexicon,* ed. I. Bekker. Berlin, 1854.

Tacitus. *C. Taciti Annales,* ed. H. Furneaux. 2nd ed. 2 vols. Oxford, 1896-1907.

Thalheim, T. "Antomosia" and "Diomosia," *RE*.
Thucydides. *Thucydidis Historiae,* eds. H. Stuart Jones and J. E. Powell. 2nd ed. 2 vols. Oxford, 1963.
Tod, M. N. *A Selection of Greek Historical Inscriptions*. 2 vols. Oxford, 1946-48.
———. *International Arbitration amongst the Greeks*. Oxford, 1913.
Toumbouros, G. *Parallel Legislations*. Vol. 1 (The Laws of Ancient Greece). Munich, 1959.
Van Cleef, F. L. "Index Antiphonicus," *CSCP*, no. 5, 1895.
Van Effenterre, H. "A propos du Serment des Drériens," *Bulletin de Correspondence Hellénique*, vol. 61 (1937).
Vinogradoff, P. *Outlines of Historical Jurisprudence*. Vol. 2 (The Jurisprudence of the Greek City). Oxford, 1922.
Wade-Gery, H. T. *Essays in Greek History*. Oxford, 1958.
Willetts, H. C. *Aristocratic Society in Ancient Crete*. London, 1955.
Wolf, E. *Griechisches Rechtsdenken*. Frankfort, 1956.
Wolff, H. F. "The Origin of Judicial Litigation among the Greeks," *Traditio* IV (1946).
Xenophon. *Xenophontis Opera*, ed. E. C. Marchant. 5 vols. Oxford, 1901-20.
Xenophon, Pseudo—. *Athenaion Politeia*, ed. E. Kalinka. Leipzig, 1934.
Ziebarth, E. *De Jurejurando in Jure Graeco Quaestiones*. Göttingen, 1892 (diss.).
———. "Eid," *RE*.
Zimmern, A. F. *The Greek Commonwealth*. 5th ed. Oxford, 1931.

Index